The Night the FITZ Went Down

by Hugh E. Bishop

in cooperation with
Dudley Paquet

Lake Superior Port Cities Inc.

First Edition: August 2000

 LAKE SUPERIOR PORT CITIES INC.
P.O. Box 16417
Duluth, Minnesota 55816-0417
USA
888-BIG LAKE (244-5253) • www.lakesuperior.com

Publishers of *Lake Superior Magazine* and *Lake Superior Travel Guide*

5 4 3 2

Bishop, Hugh E., 1940-
    The night the Fitz went down / by Hugh E. Bishop. – 1st ed.
        p. cm.
    Includes bibliographical references and index.
    ISBN 0-942235-37-1 (pbk.)
    1. Edmund Fitzgerald (Ship) 2. Shipwrecks – Superior, Lake. I. Title

G530.E26 B57 2000
363.1'23'097749-dc21   00-030459

Printed in the United States of America

    Editors: Paul L. Hayden, Konnie LeMay
    Designers: Mathew Pawlak, Jillene Johnson
        Printer: Cushing-Malloy Inc., Ann Arbor, Michigan

Dedication

To the Great Lakes Captains
and the Crews they guide

Foreword

Jim Marshall

When I first met Captain Dudley Paquette about 10 years ago, he was introduced to me by a mutual seagoing friend as a weather wizard. I absorbed that bit of information, thinking smugly, "Sure. He and every other Great Lakes sailor."

It didn't take long before I realized that Dudley does have a special talent in weather prognostication and, as a pleasure boater on Lake Superior, I came to value his nautical advice and weather savvy – as well as his friendship and camaraderie. I also came to realize that his experience in the monstrous storm of November 9-10, 1975, had possibilities for an interesting and enduring story.

Thus, I get to the meat of this book, in which Captain Paquette gives the most detailed eyewitness account of the *Edmund Fitzgerald* storm that I've seen or heard, along with an outstanding narrative of the events surrounding his own trip through that storm. Interwoven into that description are his thoughts on the loss of the *Fitz* and his analysis that a miscalculation of the severity of the storm was one of the major contributing factors in the wreck of the *Fitzgerald*. Author Hugh Bishop has taken Captain Paquette's theory and investigated, finding that there are numerous points of support, making this all the more fascinating a study.

While Captain Paquette is supremely confident in his interpretation of the cause of the wreck and presents a compelling case that the sinking of November 10, 1975, was the culmination of several critical factors, there is probably no way that any theory can be proved or disproved as to the cause of the wreck. With no survivors or eyewitnesses to the sudden disappearance of the big freighter, nearly any explanation has as much credibility as any other. There have been any number of explanations made, for the subject of the sinking continues to be as mysterious today as it was 25 years ago.

Unlike earlier Great Lakes wrecks, interest in the *Fitzgerald* has not diminished as years passed. Indeed, there are probably more people today with intense interest in the wreck than there were just after the sinking. Captain Paquette's insights and vast knowledge of the shipping industry will generate new information, new questions and yet more material for discussion.

James R. Marshall

Contents

Introduction

From the standpoint of a descriptive narration, perhaps the "Findings of Fact" by the Marine Board of Investigation to the commandant of the U.S. Coast Guard is as succinct as anything written about the November 10, 1975, wreck of the SS *Edmund Fitzgerald*:

"In the early evening of 10 November 1975, the SS Edmund Fitzgerald, *while in a severe storm, with a full cargo of taconite pellets, sank in eastern Lake Superior at 46°59.9'N, 85°06.6'W, approximately 17 miles from the entrance to Whitefish Bay, MI.* Fitzgerald *had left Superior, WI, on the afternoon of 9 November en route Detroit, MI, and was in communication with other vessels periodically throughout the voyage. At approximately 1530, 10 November,* Fitzgerald *reported some topside damage and a list but did not say what caused this damage or express any urgency in the report. The Master of* Fitzgerald *did request that the steamer* Arthur M. Anderson, *which was following, provide navigational information to* Fitzgerald *and, as the two vessels proceeded toward Whitefish Bay,* Fitzgerald *disappeared from* Anderson's *radar screen.*

"No distress message was received from Fitzgerald. *The notification from* Anderson *of the suspected loss precipitated an extensive air and surface search. A large quantity of debris, including lifeboats, life rafts and other flotsam, was found, but no survivors or bodies were recovered. All of the 29 crewmen on board at the time are missing."*

* * *

Captain Dudley J. Paquette was a happy master, after taking command of Inland Steel Company's SS Wilfred Sykes. He loaded opposite the Edmund Fitzgerald in Superior, Wisconsin, on November 9, 1975.

"For your sake, Cap, you better be right about this big blow you're expecting," warned Second Mate Lee Ward, as he gazed out the pilothouse windows of the 678-foot Inland Steel Company ore freighter SS *Wilfred Sykes* at an unusually nice November afternoon in Superior, Wisconsin. "If you're wrong, this longer trip will spell one helluva hot gale blowing right in your face from the fleet office down Chicago way."

"Oh, there's a storm brewing all right. It's just a question of when it'll hit and how bad it'll get," replied Captain Dudley Paquette, a veteran of a quarter-century as an officer or master on Great Lakes ships – yet lacking three years to his 50th birthday.

About 24 hours earlier, on their upbound trip from Indiana Harbor, Indiana, just southeast of Chicago, he'd begun following and charting information on a low pressure system that began marching northeasterly from Oklahoma toward Lake Superior on November 8, 1975. The Weather Service long range forecast originally predicted that the storm would pass just south of Lake Superior, but his own chart did not convince him of that route and, by 7 a.m. November 9, the forecast had been amended to indicate that the system would cross Lake Superior east of Michipicoten Island at the eastern shore.

What he had witnessed and analyzed of the storm system now resulted in his decision to take the long road home. He looked

Originally a straight decker, the Wilfred Sykes *was re-equipped as a self-unloader (opposite page) by Fraser Shipyards Inc. in Superior, Wisconsin, the winter before the wreck of the* Edmund Fitzgerald.

again at the running weather chart that was always present and updated in the pilothouse on every boat he mastered. All of his experience and weather training reassured him in his decision to stick with the detour he'd charted along Lake Superior's Minnesota north shore, through the 16-mile-wide channel between Isle Royale and the Ontario north shore, and the possibility of protected anchorage behind the Sleeping Giant in Thunder Bay, Ontario, if this major storm created the havoc he expected.

"Every sailor knows you'll get some heavy weather," Captain Paquette says. "As a captain in their fleet, Inland Steel paid me to deliver ore. I was nothing if not a helluva super company man and believed in getting the cargo to its destination as quickly and inexpensively as possible, but I never believed they expected me to take risks. A few hours of extra sailing time to prevent damage to the ship on one trip wouldn't ruin the season and it might just save the company a lot of money, if anything went wrong."

The previous winter, the *Sykes* had undergone major retrofitting at Fraser Shipyards in Superior to convert the vessel into a self-unloader capable of off-loading taconite pellets by a system of gates and belts in the cargo hold that delivers the ore to the dock from a boom that swings out over the side of the boat and dock. After shipyard work was completed, the *Sykes* went back into service in June of this 1975 shipping season.

In addition to his instinct about this weather system, Captain Paquette had weighed the fact that the newly converted self-

unloader had not faced a major Lake Superior storm since the additional weight of the self-unloading equipment and topside boom was added. Although his experience thus far was that the ship was even sturdier than it had been before the conversion and despite the fact that he had every confidence in any ship on which he served, he opted not to test this November storm, which had shown all the early symptoms of a major system.

The SS *Edmund Fitzgerald* had finished loading at the east side of the Burlington Northern Dock #1 opposite the *Sykes* and departed a couple of hours earlier. From his pilothouse, Captain Paquette watched that famous Great Lakes ore carrier, nicknamed "the Big *Fitz*" by sailors, back away from the dock as soon as the last loading spout was clear, make a sharp turn and steam out through the Superior Entry, its deck crew moving and placing hatch covers over the cargo hold as the ship entered Lake Superior's placid, rippleless waters.

"Doesn't even take time to get the hatches closed before he's ringing full speed ahead," one of the pilothouse crew noted dryly.

Captain Paquette nodded. The *Fitzgerald*'s reputation as a ship in a hurry was well-known in Great Lakes shipping circles, but he had his own vessel to tend to and turned his attention to the deck, where loading was taking place under the supervision of veteran First Mate Russ Carlson.

At about 4 p.m., the Weather Service came on with a report that the storm path was now forecast to cross the lake during the next 12 to 24 hours from the Keweenaw Peninsula of Upper Michigan, traveling northeastward into Ontario in the area of Michipicoten Island. His own analysis agreed with the Weather

Service that the low pressure system was deepening and would turn into ugly weather later that evening. His only quibble was that he was not convinced that the Weather Service had the route of the storm exactly right.

"If they were right about the storm passing over the Keweenaw, we'd run into mainly moderate southeast and southerly winds at the edge of the storm," he says. "If the storm passed further to the east, we'd encounter east and northeast winds and we could expect them to be much more severe and that was what I believed we were actually seeing develop on our weather chart."

As they topped off the *Sykes'* holds, moved hatch covers into place and turned for departure from the Superior Entry at 1615 (4:15 p.m.) on their downbound trip, the pilothouse crew listened with interest to conversation between captains Ernest McSorley of the *Fitzgerald* and Jesse B. "Bernie" Cooper on the SS *Arthur M. Anderson*, which departed Two Harbors, Minnesota, about 10 miles ahead of the *Fitzgerald* shortly before the *Sykes* sailed from Superior.

Looking at nearly perfect weather, the masters of the *Fitzgerald* and *Anderson* discussed whether the weather advisories that were being broadcast by the U.S. Weather Service were significant. By the end of the conversation, Cooper and McSorley agreed that they'd stick to the regular Lake Carriers' Association downbound route, which would take them northeast to a point just off the Keweenaw Peninsula, where they expected to encounter the leading edge of the storm system.

The decision to take the usual route to the Soo by these two veteran captains likely added to the quiet in the wheelhouse as the *Sykes* churned the smooth waters off Minnesota's north shore on the first leg of its journey. Paquette caught the questioning looks not only of Ward, but first and third mates Carlson and Peter Plimpton, as they calculated how long the "Old Man" would stick to this roundabout route in the face of such nice weather. Calmly, he told them to be sure that everything was battened down and to double check anything they weren't dead certain about.

"We talked about the weather forecast in the off-hand manner that is common on the bridges of Great Lakes freighters – after all, weather just goes with this job – but ever since I first made captain 11 years before, I had insisted that my mates monitor weather reports and record all the pertinent information on our running weather chart in the pilothouse. We were an official weather reporting ship, so we had our own equipment to fill in any additional information that we observed and I had a pretty complete picture of this weather system in my mind. I didn't always believe the Weather Service forecasts, especially when they went out beyond 12 hours and especially in November, but this time, my own analysis agreed with their forecast of severe weather. I just wasn't confident of their forecast that the storm was tracking in a pattern to pass to the northeast over the Keweenaw.

"November always brings the most treacherous weather on the Great Lakes and that's even more true of Lake Superior. I could see from our charts that we had all the early signs that this was going to be a serious storm and I saw no reason to challenge such a system. I also wondered why the captains of the *Fitzgerald* and *Anderson* chose to ignore the forecast and to sail right into the teeth of it.

"Still, you never know about Great Lakes weather in November, so I told my officers that we'd continue on my north shore course until the 2000 (8 p.m.) weather report, when we could update the barometric readings on our chart, draw in new isobars and plot the progress of this low pressure system more accurately.

"As we closed with the north shore and passed Two Harbors, the 1800 weather forecast was upgraded to gale warnings and still predicted that the Keweenaw would be the crossing point. The front had crossed the border between northeastern Iowa and southwest Wisconsin traveling northeastward at 30 to 40 miles per hour. I knew we'd be seeing the effects of that low pressure system before long."

But the tracking information in that report confirmed Captain Paquette's earlier analysis that the storm center was headed farther to the east. This deepening low would create a counter-clockwise pattern of winds west of that crossing track that would be devastating as they gathered force across the full expanse of Lake Superior from the east and northeast.

"I became convinced that the north shore course was the right decision and that the central and western portions of Lake Superior were about to see all of the power that a November northeaster is famous for," the captain says. When the 2000 (8 p.m.) report came through, it confirmed his decision to stay on the north shore. Gale warnings were repeated for the lake and life aboard any vessel that was under way would become increasingly uncomfortable.

"We had no clue at this point just how uncomfortable it was to be, but a matter of hours would prove again that Lake Superior is a sea that you can love completely, but never trust."

Eavesdropping on Disaster

*The Commandant concurred with the Marine Board that the most
probable cause of the sinking was the loss of buoyancy resulting from the
massive flooding of the cargo hold. This flooding most likely took place
through ineffective hatch closures. The vessel dove into a wall of water
and never recovered, with the breaking up of the ship occurring as it
plunged or as the ship struck the bottom.*

Excerpt from Title Page
U.S. Coast Guard Marine Board of Investigation Report

*It should be emphasized that the proximate cause of the sinking could
not be determined, so any theoretical rationale advanced could only be
a* possible *cause.... The present hatch covers are an advanced design
and are considered by the entire lake shipping industry to be a most
significant improvement over the telescoping leaf covers previously used
for many years. The one-piece covers have proven completely satisfactory
in all weather operations without a single vessel loss in almost 40 years
of use. Closure clamps have been greatly improved over the years to the
present cast steel clamps that have also been found to be completely
satisfactory in service.... If ineffective closings exist, as alleged by the
Coast Guard, surely during the 40 years operating experience there
would have been watery cargo to unload, be it ore, coal, grain or stone.
This not only would have been readily apparent, but also a costly
problem that vessel and cargo owners would not tolerate. If significant
water did enter the cargo holds in this manner during a downbound
voyage, there would be a corresponding change in draft. Draft readings
are recorded by the vessel before leaving the loading port, by the Corps*

*of Engineers at the Soo Locks and by the vessel upon arrival at the
unloading port. Periodically, the Coast Guard checks the drafts. There
are few unexplained changes that have occurred en route, and none of
these were accompanied by water accumulation in the cargo holds …
in almost 40 years of experience.*

Excerpt of Sept. 16, 1977, letter to
National Transportation Safety Board from
U.S.C.G. Vice Admiral (Ret.) Paul Trimble, President
Lake Carriers' Association, Cleveland, Ohio

Comfortably seated in front of a large bank of windows
overlooking the shoreline of his summer home on Lake
Vermilion in northeastern Minnesota, Captain Dudley Paquette
(retired, 1980, Inland Steel Company fleet) looks back on the
events of those fateful two or three days surrounding the 1975
sinking of the SS *Edmund Fitzgerald* and scoffs at the U.S. Coast
Guard's Marine Board of Investigation conclusion that "ineffective
hatch closures" was the primary cause of flooding that led to the
sinking of the *Edmund Fitzgerald*.

"To put it plain and simple, that's just bull," he says. "In their
underwater photographs, they found clamps with no evidence of

U.S. COAST GUARD

*Hatch clamps have threaded buttons to allow adjustments that maintain
pressure on the hatch covers when the clamps are dogged down. The photo of
undogged, undamaged clamps at left is an underwater shot on the Fitzgerald.*

Snug and seaworthy, the SS Edward L. Ryerson shows all hatch clamps securely fastened as it heads down the lake with a load of taconite pellets bound for Indiana Harbor, Indiana.

damage and concluded that was evidence that they were improperly adjusted and did not seal the cover down, but I'd be more inclined to think that those clamps were never even fastened, because I watched the deck crew putting the covers in place when the ship headed out into Lake Superior from Superior Entry. Besides, even if some clamps aren't properly adjusted or clamped down on a hatch cover, I know damned good and well that those patented hatch covers won't leak enough water into the hold to jeopardize a ship like the *Fitz.*"

The modern patent hatch covers and clamping system that Captain Paquette's describing consist of a single piece of shaped steel plate, with gasketing at the closure point of the cover where it is clamped to the top of coamings (the 24-inch high, watertight vertical borders around the *Fitzgerald's* hatch openings). These covers are fastened to the hatch coamings by double-action clamps fixed on the coamings. When properly adjusted to exert tension on the hatch cover, the clamps require a substantial downward force to snap the handle into place, locking the cover to the coaming. Each clamp had a threaded adjusting bolt that could be turned to increase or decrease tension on the cover and also dictated the amount of exertion required to snap the clamp shut. On the *Fitzgerald*, each hatch had 68 clamps to seal the covers to the coamings.

The *Fitzgerald's* hatch covers were made of $^5/_{16}$-inch steel plate, were 11 feet 7 inches wide, 54 feet long and weighed seven tons each. To move the covers on or off the hatches, their weight requires that the ships have large cranes (called "iron deckhands" by the sailors) that are mounted on rails and travel the length of the main deck where the hatch openings are located. Captain Paquette says that, even if several clamps were improperly adjusted, this system would still keep out water in very large seas. "I've just never believed that the Coast Guard got close to finding the real cause of the wreck," he summarizes the hatch cover explanation.

He pauses and remembers, "When I was a deckhand in my first job on the old SS *Chacornac* in 1943, we lost a couple of the old telescoping hatch covers – actually, they fell into the hold on top of the coal we were hauling and we had a helluva time getting them back up to cover the hatches. We took on a lot of water while we were covering those hatches back up and getting the tarps over them, but we were never in danger of sinking – and the *Chacornac* was tiny in comparison to a boat the size of the *Fitz*.

"No – the Coast Guard's *investigation* was okay, but their *conclusion* that the hatch covers or clamps were defective and let in enough water to cause the ship to sink just never held water with me, if you'll pardon a joke," says Captain Paquette with a smile.

After the wreck, it was a constant topic of discussion wherever sailors and Lake Superior denizens met, and several theories about the sinking developed – though Paquette's opinion about leaky hatch covers was pretty much the standard judgment among sailors.

A theory that gained much wider acceptance was that the *Fitzgerald* struck the Six-Fathom Shoal that lurks at and extends some distance north and east from the north end of Caribou Island off the eastern shoreline of Lake Superior (this is also called "grounding," "shoaling" or having "shoaled"). This theory has the ship being either severely punctured ("holed") or suffering critical structural damage that left it at the mercy of the raging seas.

To better understand this theory, it is useful to know that the ship had eight ballast tanks located outside of and under the cargo holds, effectively giving the ship a double bottom. Ballast tanks are divided at the center or keel line in the bottom of the hull and are numbered as port (left) or starboard (right) Number 1, 2, etc., beginning at the bow. When the ship is light (carrying no cargo), water is pumped into these tanks to provide ballast (weight) that stabilizes the ship and keeps the propeller in the water. Each of the tanks had two eight-inch vent pipes that extended through the weather or spar deck where the hatch openings were located. These vents allowed air to escape the tank as water was pumped in and

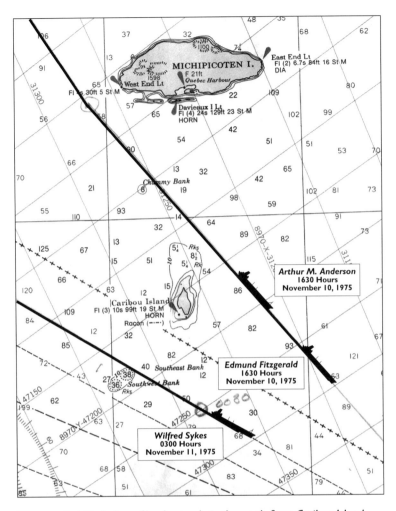

The so-called Six-Fathom Shoal extends to the north from Caribou Island.
One theory about the loss of the Fitzgerald is that it struck the shoals, was
damaged and began to take on water that eventually sank the ship.

were capped 18 inches above the deck with an adjustable cap that
could be closed to provide watertight security, although there was
no visible indicator of open or closed positions.

In his 1987 book, *Shipwrecks of Lake Superior*, James R. Marshall
was one of the early popularizers of the shoaling theory.

Based on extensive research and conversations with Captain
Bernie Cooper of the SS *Arthur M. Anderson*, Marshall published
the following account: "The official findings of the Coast Guard

refute her (the *Fitzgerald*) striking the shoal, but for the sake of conjecture, let us assume for the moment she did, indeed, find the shoal, which damaged her (ballast) tanks to a fatal degree.... Those aboard, amid the din of high wind and rushing seas, might not have known it. In such sea conditions, pounding becomes an ever-present condition, hardly noted after a while, if other problems preoccupy one's thoughts.

"Assuming the grounding, (the ship) would have 'hogged,' in the parlance of the lakes. Both the bow and stern, not being supported by the shoal, would have bent downward, raising the mid or supported section. The first equipment to react would be the cable fences along the edge of the deck. They would tighten and finally fail from the strain. Whether the straining three strands of cable could have torn at or dislodged the tank vents is pure conjecture, not worthy of discussion beyond the comments made in Captain McSorley's next radio transmission (in which) Captain McSorley reported to the *Anderson* that his ship 'a fence rail down, two (ballast tank) vents damaged and a list.' To mariners, a list means the vessel no longer rides evenly, but leans to one side or the other. McSorley added that he would slow down to allow the *Anderson* to catch up and keep track of her.

"In response to Captain Cooper's question, McSorley acknowledged that he had his pumps going. 'Yes,' he said, 'both of them....'

"Only one logical conclusion remains: when McSorley spoke of 'both' pumps, he meant that he had started two pumps to remove water from the ballast tanks, NOT THE CARGO HOLD."[1]

The *Fitzgerald* had a total of six electric pumps to fill or drain the ballast tanks that could also be used to evacuate water from the cargo hold via a collection well in the rear hold. Four main pumps were each rated at 7,000 gallons a minute capacity and two auxiliary electric pumps were each capable of pumping 2,000 gallons a minute. Assuming that the two pumps McSorley started were of the larger volume, he was pumping 14,000 gallons a minute, which apparently did not correct the list.

As support for the shoaling/holing theory, proponents point to Captain Bernie Cooper's testimony during the Coast Guard's Marine Board of Investigation hearings that the *Anderson*'s radar showed the *Fitzgerald* to be closer to the shoal than Cooper wanted the *Anderson* to be. Also lending credence were the results of a re-survey of the shoal after the wreck, which showed that it extends about a mile farther east (the side on which both ships passed) than

INLAND STEEL COMPANY
GENERAL OFFICES

DATE   November 12, 1975

TO   Riley O'Brien
TITLE   Fleet Manager   FROM
DEPT.   General Office - 18
                                                     TITLE   Captain
                                                     DEPT.   Str. Wilfred Sykes
COPIES TO   FILE REF.

SUBJECT   TRIP # 38

                    DOWNBOUND - FROM - SUPERIOR, WIS.

The Str. Edmund Fitzgerald, loaded East #1 at Allouez, dept.
approx. two and one half (2½) hours ahead of this ship, which dept.
Superior Piers at 1637 on November 9, 1975. The wind was NE heavy,
my heading was 45 degree's true course to the knife river haul. Than
set a course of 57 Degree's true, along the North shore of Lake
Superior. At 0305 November 10, 1975, I reduced speed, heavy NNE
seas and Gale force winds. My position, Rock of Ages, North Side.

At 0320 November 10, 1975, the Second Mate tried to contact
the "Fitzgerald". No contact made. But a few minutes later, the Arthur
Anderson made contact with the "Fitzgerald" and the conversation was
as follows -
          From the vicinity of Eagle Harbor, "Anderson" steering 055
degree's for a point 10 miles South of Slate Island. Wind - 042 degree's
50 - 60 Knots Heavy Seas. Fitzgerald steering 035 degree's checked
down. Fitzgerald questioned "Anderson's" speed. Second Mate, again
tried to contact "Fitzgerald", but the "Anderson" came in and repeated
the above sea and wind conditions.

I proceeded into Thunder Bay, anchoring at 0830 November
10, 1975. Wind - North at 50 - 60 Knots in gusts.
          The wind kept coming around to the NW and after receiving
the Canadian weather - Ship - Station reports, I hove up anchor at
1245 arriving Passage Isld. at 1536 - Wind 290 degree's 35 - 40 Knots.
I proceeded downbound along with the Str. Roger Blough, arriving the
disaster area at 0300 November 11, 1975. Received orders from the U.S.
Coast Guard - Soo, Mich. to check down, await daylight, than search for
survivers. I was released from the area at 1300 same date, than con't.
downbound for the Soo.

Captain Paquette's letter to Inland fleet manager Riley O'Brien on November 12, 1975, succinctly describes events during the November 9-10 "storm of the century."

charts of the time indicated. Significantly, within about 15 minutes of passing the shoal, Paquette heard McSorley report the damage, saying he was "making water in the #7 ballast tank" (the hinge area). In his testimony, Cooper is quoted as saying, "He took that list, which seemed to be real fast."

And, indeed, in the letter written to the National Transportation Safety Board after the Coast Guard Board's findings were released, the Lake Carriers' Association, whose members are the companies that own or operate boats on the Great Lakes, stated that the shoaling theory was the "only readily explained" reason for the sudden list and the volume of water being pumped.[2]

Captain Paquette is less scornful of this explanation than he is of the ineffective hatch cover theory, but still thinks it unlikely.

"Captain McSorley was not a master that I admired, but he sure wasn't some rookie in an unfamiliar area making his first run in heavy seas," Paquette says. "He had certainly used the

Captain Dudley J. Paquette

north route dozens of times in his 25 years as a master and he would also have navigated many times in snow squalls, fog and other limited visibility. I just don't believe he would allow his ship near a shoal that was known to be dangerous by every navigator on the lakes."

Captain Jimmie Hobaugh, commander of the U.S. Coast Guard cutter *Woodrush* that set sail from Duluth, Minnesota, the evening of November 10 and pounded through seas for 22 hours to the wreck site agrees that the veteran captain of the *Fitzgerald* was not likely to have stumbled onto the Six-Fathom Shoal, although his other observations on the sinking diverge from those of Captain Paquette, as will be examined later.

Asked why he is so skeptical of both the hatch clamp and the shoaling theories, Paquette says, "The LCA's letter pretty well destroyed the Coast Guard's explanation that failure of the hatch covers caused the wreck, but it does support the shoaling theory, saying it was 'the only' cause for the list and other damage that was reported by McSorley a few minutes after his ship passed Caribou.

"I'll be the first to admit that I believe the LCA is absolutely right about the hatch covers, but I don't believe that shoaling is the only other explanation, as they say," he says, pointing out that the deep diving photo expeditions by the Coast Guard right after the wreck and the one in 1994 led by Frederick Shannon (*Michigan Natural Resources Magazine*, December 1995) showed the bottom of the overturned stern section quite clearly. In none of these photos is there any sign of scraping or other evidence of having hit the shoals. There is no puncture visible on any portion of the bottom and no damage to either the propeller or the rudder to support the shoaling theory.

In addition, Captain Hobaugh points out and Frederick Stonehouse states in his best selling book, *The Wreck of the* Edmund Fitzgerald, that divers searched the Six-Fathom Shoal after the wreck and found no sign that there had been a recent collision or grounding anywhere on the shoal.

"I think the LCA was just putting out a smoke screen with the shoaling theory," Paquette says, then explains what he means. "The LCA works for the interest of shipping companies and it wasn't in their interest, or anyone else's for that matter, to redesign hatch covers that had proven to be perfectly safe in every kind of weather during 40 years of use. By making a strong case that the sinking was caused by damage from striking the Six-Fathom Shoal, they diverted attention from other explanations – like the possibility that something about the boat itself or the handling of the ship during the storm might have been the reason she sank. That would have been a huge headache for the LCA companies, the Coast Guard and American Bureau of Shipping. If anything suggested that the ship or the captain's shiphandling was suspect, everybody from the unions to the government would have been after the companies and it would have destroyed confidence in the safety of Great Lakes shipping."

* * *

But Captain Paquette had full confidence in the SS *Wilfred Sykes* by the time he watched that low pressure system moving toward Lake Superior from the southwest, building into the November 9-10 "storm of the century." The ship had been sailing since coming out of Fraser Shipyards in Superior, Wisconsin, the previous June, having had a self-unloading system installed that added tons of new steel to what had already been a sturdy superstructure.

"If I could pick any ship to be on in that storm, the *Sykes* would be my choice," the captain says. "But I'm still thankful I had the weather training and experience to stay on the north shore route when we left the dock at Superior on November 9."

Having made the decision to track Lake Superior's Minnesota and Ontario north shore, Captain Dudley Paquette and his shipmates enjoyed smooth sailing during the early hours of their northeastward trip.

"The Weather Service's first prediction that the storm center would pass south of the lake on the night of November 9-10 was corrected well before the storm front entered the area and I was sure the path of the storm would be at the eastern end of the lake," Paquette says. "It actually ended up passing over Marquette, well to the east. The barometric readings that we had been charting showed that this was developing into a major storm rolling toward the area from the southwest, but there was nothing odd or different about the pattern of this storm. It had the typical counter-clockwise rotation you'd expect and we knew we'd be seeing the wind on the western lake rotating around from the east to the northeast, north and finally coming around from the west.

"The *Anderson* and the *Fitz* were sailing in good weather right into the predicted route of the storm front, if it passed over the Keweenaw like predicted. My chart convinced me that the route the Weather Service predicted for the storm was wrong – but I doubt that many captains took enough interest in studying weather to question what the Weather Service predicted. Most of them would only worry about weather if it looked like it was going to slow them down.

"But McSorley didn't make his decision alone. Captain Bernie Cooper on the *Anderson* was ahead of the *Fitz* from Two Harbors up past Isle Royale and sailed the same route as McSorley throughout the trip. They convinced each other that what they were seeing was not as serious as the Weather Service was predicting – and all of us were very aware of that unwritten threat to replace a captain whose costs or delays got out of hand."

Captain Paquette says that he listened to the early evening conversations as the two captains agreed to stick with the normal shipping lane to the tip of the Keweenaw Peninsula and seek shelter on the southeast shore of the Keweenaw, if they found the increasing winds that could be expected when the front of the low pressure system blew in.

"But anyone who knows weather would know they'd be trapped down there as the rotation of the storm system brought the wind around to southeast, then the east and northeast. In a northeast wind, they'd take a pounding on the southeast side of the Keweenaw, so that was a flawed plan right from the start. But, again, I just don't think they were worried by the weather reports and McSorley believed his ship would handle anything, so he just charged full speed ahead into it. By the time they realized it was a monster storm, all they could do was turn north and try for lee, an area sheltered from wind and waves, on the Canadian shore. By then, that route exposed them to the worst of the storm on every

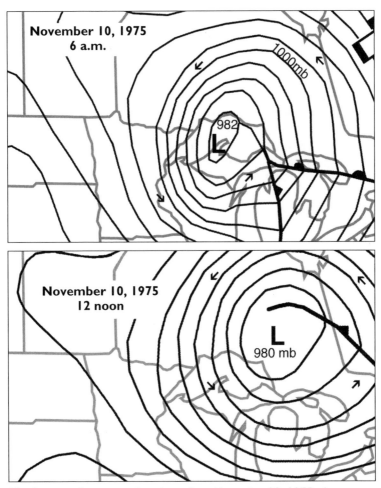

The 6 a.m. and noon weather charts from November 10, 1975, show dramatic low pressure and the shifting pattern of the wind, which blew first from the northeast, then swung to the northwest.

leg of their voyage – the worst of the northeaster, then the worst of the northwest seas when the wind came around from the northwest."

As dusk darkened into night, the wind freshened from the south, slowly whirling to the southeast, east and northeast, gathering force as the inexorable counter-clockwise atmospheric rotation gave the wind the full expanse of Lake Superior's east-west axis to gather force.

"A small U.S. Steel boat was running on the open lake to our starboard and, when the wind started coming up and he saw us hugging the north shore, he ducked in behind me. I never did figure out what boat it was or where he went, but I think when he saw us hugging the shore, he decided he'd be better off taking our example, because we were a helluva lot bigger boat than he was."

At last light, the officers and deck crew had inspected the *Sykes* one last time, ensuring that everything was secure and shipshape, then returned to their routine and waited as the evening hours accumulated and the force of the wind increased and shifted toward the northeast. The storm front now proved to be heading northeastward over Marquette to the Slate Islands and Marathon, Ontario, considerably east of the revised forecast that it would bisect the lake over the Keweenaw Peninsula. This let the storm gain energy over open water. The easterly, then northeasterly, winds gathered fury as they blew toward the *Sykes* across the cold waters of Lake Superior.

The radar glowed in the darkened pilothouse and the vague shadows of Isle Royale and Rock of Ages light blipped at the edge of the long range setting as they proceeded along the north shore. The ship was beginning to roll and the men in the pilothouse were steadying themselves as the deck of the pilothouse danced to the rhythm of increasing seas.

"Our own safety was our first concern, of course, but as we listened to their radio conversations, I couldn't help imagining the *Anderson* and *Fitz* out there on the open lake and exposed to much worse conditions," Captain Paquette remembers.

Those conversations from the main shipping lane took increasing note of wind, rising seas and snow squalls. Paquette's instinct, years of weather training, observation and two previous days of mapping this low pressure weather system combined to tell him that subsequent conversations would increase in intensity.

"The barometer's dropping," Paquette told the watch officer. "This is going to be a big storm all right, and I wouldn't want to be those guys out there."

As the northeast winds stiffened, Captain Paquette's course kept the *Sykes* within five miles or so of the north shore and they approached the passage between the north shore and Isle Royale.

"Our wind indicating equipment showed a northeast wind of 38 nautical miles per hour but, by the time we had logged this information on our weather board, it had increased to the mid-40s – easily meeting the definition of a strong gale. Sometime during that night, we got a weather report that said a station in upper Michigan reported the lowest barometric reading ever seen in the

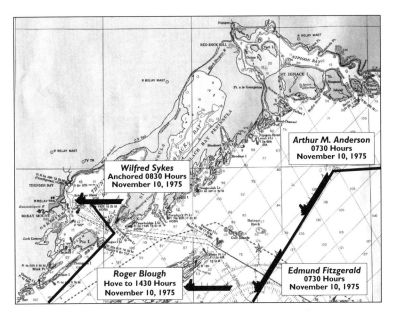

Arthur M. Anderson
0730 Hours
November 10, 1975

Wilfred Sykes
Anchored 0830 Hours
November 10, 1975

Roger Blough
Hove to 1430 Hours
November 10, 1975

Edmund Fitzgerald
0730 Hours
November 10, 1975

By about 2 a.m. on November 10, 1975, Captain Paquette was experiencing heavy going, as northeast winds piled water into the channel between Isle Royale and the Lake Superior north shore.

United States and I believe it, because our own readings just kept dropping through the rest of the trip along the shore."

By the time the second mate called in the midnight weather report, required of all official weather reporting ships, which the *Sykes* was, decreasing barometric pressure, increasing wind velocity and the rotation of wind direction reaffirmed his belief that worse weather was coming.

With interest, those in the pilothouse heard McSorley and Cooper agree shortly after midnight to change course from their exposed east-northeast heading off the western Keweenaw and run for hoped-for shelter of the big lake's northern and eastern shore on a course of 055 degrees (northeast by east). Obviously, the two ships were encountering increasingly bad weather and significant northeast seas.

"As we approached Rock of Ages in very heavy seas at about 0100 on November 10, with Isle Royale clearly on the radar, we entered the channel and the wind had jumped through the categories of strong gale (41-47 knots) and storm (48-55 knots) and building seas were attacking us. I called for a reduction in propeller rpms, because the full ahead speed we had been maintaining challenged the strength of the ship in these increasing seas."

Captain Paquette pauses, shakes his head and says, "I've seen my share of big storms, but when this storm started to really blow out of the northeast, we were somewhat protected in the lee of Isle Royale, but the seas still built to a size I couldn't believe."

As the seas built, Paquette says, the increasing wind was now swirling snow in blinding proportions out of the blackness.

"The seas materialized in giant waves that cleared the bow and washed the pilothouse windows with a gushing sound that I had never heard before. Since the pilothouse is 35 feet above the normal waterline and the tops of the waves were blowing against our windows, it's easy to say that this was one of the worst storms I was ever in," he says.

Radar confirmed their position to be northwest of Rock of Ages light at the southwest end of Isle Royale when the marine radio came to life and McSorley and Cooper again spoke. Knowing the two ships to be about eight hours from the hoped-for lee of the Canadian north shore and Slate Islands, Captain Paquette and the others in the pilothouse heard McSorley confirm to Cooper that he was steering 035 degrees (northeast by north), but that his ship was working so much that he had reduced his rpms to 55. He then requested to know what rpms the *Anderson* was turning. Cooper responded that he was turning 85 rpms, rather than his standard 99 rpms.

In a later conversation between the two ships, the *Sykes'* bridge was stunned to hear the captain of the *Fitzgerald* state, "We're going to try for some lee from Isle Royale. You're walking away from us anyway … I can't stay with you."

Such a remark was totally out of character for that captain and that vessel. McSorley was not known for turning aside or slowing down. Captain Paquette and his pilothouse crew exchanged questioning glances, and he felt a slight chill of foreboding, but his ears perked up at McSorley's reference to the ship "working," which he says is seaman's vernacular to describe a twisting effect that is built into the design of ships. The working (hinge) area is about two-thirds of the distance back from the bow and, while normally not a problem, Paquette sensed that the comment and the query about the other ship's rpms masked a concern that was not evident in McSorley's calm voice.

"I turned to Lee Ward, who was on the midnight watch, and said, 'That guy is going to get into trouble!'" Paquette states. "No captain ever reveals very much on the radio and what he said wouldn't mean a helluva lot to most people, but I just had a feeling that something wasn't right when I heard that."

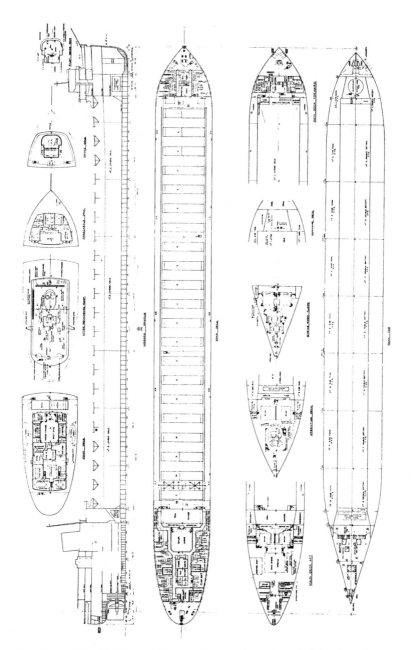

Drawings of the SS Edmund Fitzgerald *show the various deck levels and the general configuration of the ship's superstructure. The drawing at right shows the ballast tank tops in the bottom of the ship.*

Now, decades after the November 10, 1975, megastorm that wrecked the *Edmund Fitzgerald*, Captain Paquette is asked why he was so confident of his own weather instinct that he ignored the decision of two older captains and his own self-admitted interest in delivering his cargo as quickly and safely as possible. What compelled him to stick to the longer, more expensive route up Minnesota's north shore the night of November 9, thereby protecting his ship from the worst of the savage winds and seas that developed in this storm?

He grins and says, "Well, it wasn't because I was afraid of big seas. I've sailed plenty of times in waves and wind that maybe should have scared me. I was the captain and it was my decision to take the *Sykes* out of the protection of Thunder Bay later on the afternoon of November 10 and to be on the lake when the backside of that storm hit us. Believe me, the trailing seas washing over my stern and poop deck were so high they broke a strongback holding up the canvas cover on one of the lifeboats, which were about 20 to 25 feet above the normal waterline.

"I've also been in storm situations that did threaten ships I was on and, when I made captain, I never wanted to be surprised by the weather."

* * *

He looks back at his career and talks of big blows that are memorable to him.

"In 1950, I was third mate on Inland's old *Joseph L. Block* when we left Marquette, Michigan, in a northwest gale with some big waves hitting us in late fall. We had a load of natural ore that had to be thawed with steam and hot water to get it out of the ore cars and dock pockets. It was so wet and sloppy in our hold that it shifted when the ship rolled and we took a helluva list. To get back to the harbor, we had to turn into the trough of the seas and we damned near tipped over when we started taking those waves broadside.

"After we got back into the harbor, we were listing so bad the ship's spars just barely cleared the loading spouts on the dock when we tied up – and the spouts were up. We lost a week of trip time, because it took that long for the big mine pumps they brought in to get enough water out of the cargo so the ore would stay in one place in our holds."

Other especially big seas he remembers as a mate aboard Inland vessels led to the sinking of the Kinsman Transit Line's *Henry Steinbrenner* off Isle Royale in May 1953 and the grounding of the Bethlehem Steel Corporation's *Maryland* at Marquette that same year, as well as the storm that broke up and sank U.S. Steel's *Carl D. Bradley* in a November 1958 storm at Boulder Reef in Lake Michigan. Unlike the *Fitzgerald*, other ships in the area did receive emergency radio calls from the *Bradley* as it broke up and sank, but only two members of the crew survived the wreck.

As first mate on the *Philip Block* during the *Bradley* storm, Dudley Paquette remembers, "We had gone out past Gros Cap into Lake Superior, but Captain (Sidney) Ward quickly decided to go back and anchor at Waishkey Bay. It was blowing so hard it took both of our anchors to hold her in place. We could hear everything from the search and rescue effort for the *Bradley* on our radio and it was big news for weeks afterward.

"Our last trip that season was for limestone at Port Inland at the north end of Lake Michigan, and we were upbound from Indiana Harbor, Indiana, with southerly winds that turned into a southwest gale by the time we reached Point Betsie on the northwest side of the Lower Peninsula," he says. "Captain Ward decided to turn around and sail back to the west shore, which was a huge mistake because just a couple of hours would have put us at Beaver Island, where we could have easily ridden out the southwest swells. The ship was one of the first to undergo lengthening and was really limber. It was bending and twisting like crazy – I've never seen a ship work any worse than that one – but we finally made safe anchorage, waited out the storm, then proceeded to our loading point in ice and snow, got loaded and laid the boat up for the winter at Indiana Harbor."

He also remembers a storm when he was captain on the old *Joseph Block* in 1965 and encountered a spring storm between the the Keweenaw Peninsula and Passage Island at the northeast end of Isle Royale. Captain Riley Ward was a wheelman on that voyage. A veteran of 39 years of sailing and brother of the late Lee Ward, who was Paquette's second mate during the *Fitzgerald* drama, Captain Ward went on to command a number of Inland ships and retired from Inland Steel Company's fleet in 1996, then signed on as captain of the cement carrier *Alpena*. He too remembers the Passage Island storm, saying, "It was blowing a gagger, all right, especially for a little old boat like the *Joe Block*. The ship was rolling like crazy and everybody was holding onto anything that would keep them upright."

Paquette says, "I was wrapped around a radiator in the pilothouse to stay put and they tied the engineer in a chair so he stayed where he could control the rpms so we didn't bust something or shake the ship to pieces."

With these memories of intense storms, it's little wonder that as captain he wanted to know everything possible about the weather he faced, but his boyhood in Marquette, Michigan, likely provided the considerable range of weather experience on which to build his expertise. Sitting on the southern shore of Lake Superior, the city is subject to lake effects throughout the year and a virtual collage of weather conditions at any time of year. Nor'easters gather intensity during the sweep across open water and the prevailing westerlies can rage in from Lake Superior's broad expanse to the west carrying moisture from the lake that is dumped as snow to impressive depths. A natural harbor and the 1844 discovery of a nearby deposit of rich iron ore have made Marquette an important center of shipping since the 1850s. The history of the city is rife with legendary people of both nautical and financial success.

Born in 1928, the son of an unmarried, teen-aged mother and an Englishman named Seth Summerset who died before his birth, Captain Paquette was given his mother Olive's surname and was raised by his maternal grandparents. Only after he had grown in years and stature was the truth of his birth revealed to him by boyhood friends, who had heard the story whispered among adults.

"I spent years thinking my Grandma Jenny was my mother and that my mother was my sister," he says. "Evidently, when I was born, Grandma and Grandpa came to the hospital, got me and my mother and raised me as their kid. Years later, when I asked him if he wasn't embarrassed about it, Grandpa said that he was damned if he was going to hide his daughter in the basement because of a mistake she made."

And he may have inherited a scientific curiosity, since he describes his grandfather as having a wide range of interests.

"Grandpa Wesley was an interesting guy. He ran the power system for the Marquette street cars, but also built a perpetual motion machine in our basement and, once he'd get the wheel of his machine spinning, he wouldn't be able to stop it. He and Grandma kept hundreds of chickens and sold eggs. He built the Paquette Tavern in north Marquette and it supported the whole family during the Depression in the 1930s. I can still remember poker games in the front booth and, if the door wasn't open by 7 a.m., the regulars would kick it down. I believe he sold beer and wine up front, but I think that moonshine in the back room was what really paid most of the bills.

"On Friday nights, logging trucks would pull up and drop off the lumberjacks from out in the camps. They'd give Grandpa their pay checks and he kept the 'jacks entertained until 4 a.m. Monday, when he'd put them back on the trucks with a pint of moon for their trip back to the camp.

"Paquette Tavern was one of the first places in Marquette with a nickelodeon and they'd keep it stuffed with coins playing 'Sweet Violets' over and over again. My uncle, Poker Paquette, was a good baseball player and was also supposed to be the bouncer at the tavern, but he caused more trouble than anyone else. I remember Grandma raising hell with him for getting in a fight and he told her, 'I can't help it, Ma. When I punch somebody, I get a thrill that runs all the way up my arm.' I may have gotten a little of Uncle Poker's attitude, because I was never a guy who'd back down from anybody."

He laughs and says, "Grandma was determined that I would grow up to be Father Paquette and sent me to a private Catholic high school in Indiana for a year to get ready to go to seminary. Grandma and her friends were what we called First Pewers at Mass every morning, but then they'd go from church to one of their houses and play cards and have a real good time. That school and being a priest wasn't really what I saw for myself and I told the brother who ran the school that I wasn't very likely to be any good at all at celibacy, so I went back home."

Within a couple of years of his birth, Paquette's mother married. He has two half-sisters from that marriage, but he remained with his grandparents until he went sailing in 1943.

He remembers that he and his boyhood friends especially liked the winter season, when they could play hockey, but that the natural ice of the city rink was reserved for recreational skaters until 11 p.m., when the hockey kids could finally sweep and flood the rink and play until 3 or 4 a.m.

"When we were done we still had to sweep and reflood the ice for the next day, so it really got late before we'd get home. Maybe that's why standing night watch or staying on the bridge through a stormy night never really bothered me."

With this lifelong interest in weather and long experience sailing in or avoiding heavy seas, depending upon his weather expertise to make that decision, he insisted that the mates on his ships monitor all Weather Service reports and, unlike many other ships, chart the information on a weather map that was constantly updated in the pilothouse. He also attended as many courses in weather and other navigational skills as his sailing schedule allowed. He also notes that many captains of that era did not maintain ongoing weather charts nor have his interest in and the training required to accurately assess the weather information that they were receiving a day or two prior to the November 10 storm.

Indeed, in his personal account of the wreck of the *Fitzgerald* in Marshall's *Shipwrecks of Lake Superior,* the late Jesse B. "Bernie" Cooper, captain of the SS *Arthur M. Anderson*, indicates that he did not start plotting the weather conditions until 1800 (6 p.m.) on November 9, when the Weather Service ran up northeast gale warnings. At that time, Cooper says, "As is our policy, when the meteorologists become nervous, we start our own weather plots. A low pressure to the south did show on our weather plots, but it really didn't look as if it would become very drastic, just normal November low pressure."[3]

Captain Paquette nods and says, "By that time, he wouldn't have had enough of the earlier information to be able to make a very good prediction. A lot of captains just depended on what their gut instinct told them, instead of paying much attention to the weather reports. Truthfully, most of the old-time captains wouldn't know the difference between an isobar and a soda bar and just didn't bother to worry about bad weather until they ran into it. But November is the most dangerous month to sail and I took the weather reports seriously, especially those that were less than 12 hours out in the future.

"All the classes I took to complete my mate and master's license requirements were after World War II, when a lot of the techniques and equipment to accurately measure and predict weather were developed. Older officers didn't get nearly as much of that new information in their training as I did. Even when they got new equipment, they might decide it was just a doodad that cluttered up the pilothouse or they didn't take the time to attend the classes to learn what they needed to know to use it."

That his weather savvy was highly developed is recorded in the January 24, 1975, issue of Inland Steel's newspaper, in which a front page article about late winter shipping states, "When the need for navigating orders subsides, the 49-year-old master (Paquette) returns to topic number one – what weather lies ahead. Throughout the entire voyage (from Indiana Harbor to Escanaba and back), his predictions preceded the National Weather Service by six hours!"

But, Paquette notes, his weather training and experience weren't only useful in preparing for or avoiding bad weather. Occasionally, this training could be worked in his favor. One

...uly   dolla. ...-dollar are c... .... eco-   r'or the full yea. ... .9/4, In-   ...
~ce   Cent.
trip   Th.
..r at   day
'her,   ## The ◆INLAND◆ Steelmaker   "op
is   B.
.od   fin..
.ed   Vol. 21, No. 4   East Chicago, Ind.   Jan. 24, 1975   from
.dy-   Nati.
.old   TOPS C.......:.......   ...   ★★★

ga. .. orde. ...sides, one 4.. ...

old master returns to topic number one — what weather lies ahead.

All-Volunteer Crews

Throughout the entire voyage, his weather predictions accurately preceeded the National Weather Service (NWS) by six hours!

Members of the fleet participating in the extended season all are volunteers. Few regrets were voiced

Northwestern dock at the northern port until spring.

Under the direction of Capt. Dudley J. Paquette, the sleek Ryerson hit a cruising speed of just over 17 miles an hour. (Freshwater sailors don't use the "salty" term "knots.")

Top Topic: Weather Report

Understandably, discussion in the well-stocked galley was mostly

A story in the Inland Steel Company newspaper attests to the weather wisdom of Captain Dudley Paquette, who was master of the Ryerson when the author rode the ship to Escanaba, Michigan, in winter ice.

instance when weather savvy gave him an edge involved loading 35,000 tons of iron ore pellets aboard the new *Joseph L. Block* in Escanaba, Michigan. That put the draft at 29-feet 6-inches – far too deep for the ship canal at Indiana Harbor and the deepest draft to navigate that channel at that time.

(Captain Ward notes that he later took a cargo of 37,100 tons that put the draft at 31 feet into the harbor while he was captain of the *Block*, but notes that dredging had deepened some areas of the ship canal and that his monitors were showing as little as six inches of clearance in some places.)

Paquette continues, "My analysis was that we'd be sailing all the way down in a steady north wind that would push water to the south end of Lake Michigan at Indiana Harbor, where it would pile up and give me enough draft in the channel and harbor to be able to get to the dock. As insurance, I also knew that the smaller *E.J. Block* was moving materials around in the harbor and that I could use my self-unloading equipment to off-load ore to the *E.J.*, in case I was wrong and got stuck because there wasn't as much water as I figured.

"As we came in and made our turn for the dock, a tug from Great Lakes Towing Company actually came alongside and checked our draft lines, because they couldn't believe anyone would load that deep, but the tug captain gave me a big grin and waved after he saw that we were not only loaded that deep, but that we were probably going to make it to the dock without assistance. I moved the boat in as close to the dock as it'd go – maybe 20 or 25 feet away – swung deckhands onto the dock using the self-unloading boom, tied up and started dumping ore on the dock. As we lightened, I was able to use the lines to keep pulling the boat closer and closer until we were finally right against the dock."

While most of the captains of that era did not have the weather skills to pull such a stunt, he says that if they had they would certainly have exploited that knowledge, since they were promoted primarily for their willingness to push the limits in delivering cargo to the steel mills. A few hours here, a few extra tons there made considerable difference in the master's reputation with fleet management.

"It was just standard practice in those days to overload the boats and it was common in the St. Marys River to pass boats loaded so deep that their wakes were a pool of mud from the bottom," he says. "A couple of inches of extra ore on top of a cargo adds hundreds of tons of cargo on each trip. The same was pretty much true of trip-time. If you could pick up a few minutes here and there in loading and unloading or by taking a shortcut, beating another ship to the Soo Locks, second-guessing the weather or sailing with minor problems, it could add a trip or two for the season and made a difference in your career. Believe me, I know exactly how those old-timers thought and Captain McSorley was one of the masters who had a reputation for pushing his boat and as a so-called 'heavy weather captain,' which meant he'd sail in any weather."

He looks back on it and shakes his head, saying, "I met the *Fitz* many times when they were loaded and downbound in the St. Marys River and they usually had a trail of mud behind them from loading deep and pushing the rpms."

CHAPTER TWO

A Feel for the Craft

*How does the song go – "All that remains are the faces and names
of the wives and the sons and the daughters?"*

*But that isn't true, is it? There are still all of the same questions
that we had 25 years ago about what happened on the* Edmund
Fitzgerald *and how a ship that was only 18 years old just disappeared
into the lake without a sound. The rest of us kept making our rounds,
of course, sailing on and trying to let the memory of the* Edmund
Fitzgerald *fade away, but it never quite did. Even the investigations
seemed to raise more questions than they answered and a lot of us didn't
find the official reports very credible.*

Right after we searched for and found floating debris from the Fitz,
*the U.S. Coast Guard released us from our search efforts at 1300 hours
(1 p.m.) on November 11, 1975, I was captain of the first vessel
involved in the storm and the search effort to arrive at a discharge port.
A couple of the owner company's lawyers came aboard my ship at
Indiana Harbor, Indiana, and asked for my description of the
conditions in the days before the wreck and what my opinion was as to
the cause of this terrible loss. My description of those huge seas and
terrible weather took about 15 seconds and I told them that my
opinion about the wreck was that there was negligence involved. Those
lawyers hadn't even had a chance to open their briefcases, but they left
my ship in one helluva hurry when I said that. They didn't want to
hear anything about negligence.*

Captain Dudley J. Paquette
Master, SS *Wilfred Sykes*
November 1975

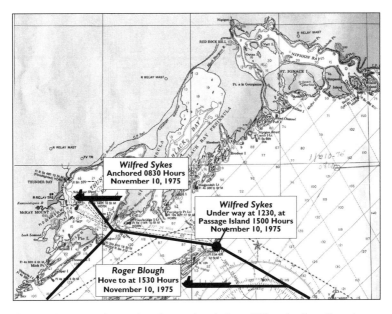

Wilfred Sykes
Anchored 0830 Hours
November 10, 1975

Wilfred Sykes
Under way at 1230, at
Passage Island 1500 Hours
November 10, 1975

Roger Blough
Hove to at 1530 Hours
November 10, 1975

Captain Paquette dropped anchor in the shelter of Thunder Bay, Ontario, at 0830 (8:30 a.m.) November 10, but was at Passage Island by about 1500 (3 p.m.) to check the seas, which had calmed as he expected.

Captain Dudley Paquette gets back to those early morning hours on November 10, 1975.

"As we continued along the north shore, our radio advised that the path of the storm center was modified and would pass over Marquette and extreme eastern Lake Superior. The advisories continued to warn of northeast, then north and then a full northwest storm for all boats sailing to the west of the storm front. My prediction had been correct and the decision to stay on the north shore was the right one. I had several options, but the *Anderson* and *Fitz* were out on the open seas and had only one option now – to run into the northeast wind and seas hoping they'd find shelter somewhere in the far reaches of the Canadian shoreline."

His own plan had always included safe anchorage behind the Sleeping Giant in the shelter of Thunder Bay (the body of water), if the storm proved to be as bad as he had predicted, but that plan would prove challenging, calling for them to run right up to the Trowbridge Island Light that marks the eastern side of the entry to

Thunder Bay, then turn just short of Trowbridge to angle into the shelter of Thunder Cape and Sibley Peninsula. With the heavy seas from the northeast, that turn would be tricky, exposing the entire 678-foot starboard side of the ship to the fury of wind and towering waves. Once inside Thunder Bay, however, the Sleeping Giant would shelter the ship from the worst of this howling nor'easter.

Paquette explains. "A vessel handles wind and waves that are striking directly on the bow quite well. That was the sea we were running in at that time. The second choice is a following sea, where the wind and water come directly at the stern of the boat. Finally, we go to some lengths to avoid 'beam seas,' where the sea and wind come directly at the side of the boat, because that creates almost pure confusion. Our present course kept the bow into the northeast wind, but the turn would fetch us broadside to the waves and wind – a big beam sea – and the weakest point in my plan."

Interestingly, in light of this explanation, the *Anderson* and *Fitzgerald* were being attacked by seas blowing at them from less than advantageous angles during much of their journey after midnight on November 9. Growing easterly winds hit them early in the storm from the starboard (right) as they traveled northeastward and came around to meet them head-on from the northeast for a period, then, after they made their turn to the east off the Canadian shoreline at about 8 a.m., the winds were rotating to the north and, when they turned on the south-southeasterly heading for Whitefish Bay at about 10 a.m. on November 10, the winds would inexorably rotate to attack them from the northwest, striking their stern from an angle off the starboard side – an oblique assault that sailors call "quartering seas."

Paquette says, "Their decision the afternoon of November 9 to ignore the weather report and stay in the regular shipping lane was a mistake that almost guaranteed they'd face heavy seas the entire trip, even after they departed from that plan later to take the longer north lane along the Canadian shoreline."

Plowing through the northeast winds and waves between Isle Royale and the Minnesota and Ontario north shore at reduced speed, the *Wilfred Sykes* continued on a course taking it ever nearer to that fateful turn at Trowbridge Island.

"As I was thinking about this, Russ Carlson, the first mate, nudged my arm and said softly, 'It's not hard to see why you're captain, Dudley. The north shore is the only place we should be tonight.'

"Russ had his master's license, so he knew what he was talking about, but any compliment like that is uncommon among officers and I accepted it with a handshake. Hardly having let go of my hand, he led me to the wind indicator and we stood there in amazement. It registered a minimum of 70 knots and the wildly swinging dial showed gusts that exceeded 100 nautical miles an hour (a nautical mile equals about 6,075 feet or 1.15 statute miles). I turned to the windows and realized that wind-driven water was easily clearing the top of the pilothouse – at least 35 feet above the waterline."

Snow and wind-driven water blotted visibility from the pilothouse to the point that they were unable to see the aft cabins – at times even obscuring sight of the steering pole extending forward from the bow directly in front of them out the pilothouse windows. The entire pilothouse crew admitted never having seen such seas.

Occasional conversation between the *Anderson* and the *Fitz* came over the radio, although a couple of attempts by Paquette's mates to speak to either the *Anderson* or *Fitz* were unsuccessful. The transmissions they picked up confirmed that the two ships were continuing to struggle on the open seas toward the Canadian shore and the Slate Islands, located well up in the northeast corner of Lake Superior, hoping to find protection there. The bridge was silent after these transmissions, although one mate did observe, "It must be a helluva note out in the open in these seas."

Just after daybreak, the *Sykes* radar picked up Trowbridge Island and Captain Paquette again told the bridge that they would run right up to Trowbridge, perhaps as close as two miles, to gain whatever shelter it and its sister islands would provide, and then turn into Thunder Bay.

He remembers, "I had to be sure that everyone understood what we were facing and talked not only to the watch on the bridge but to the chief engineer, who promised we'd have the power we'd need for the maneuver. We also warned the crew there were going to be very heavy seas.

"Later, when we talked about it, all of us in the pilothouse agreed that we got as close as we dared to Trowbridge, but none of us agreed about how much shelter we gained from those islands.

"When we went into the turn, the ship performed perfectly. Two incredible beam seas hit and rolled us to port, but all the fastenings were just as tight as the deck crew had promised and the ship came around and we were steaming with a following sea into the shelter of Thunder Cape. Everyone on the bridge broke into a grin for the first time in many hours – it had been a long night for all of us – fore and aft."

Meanwhile, at sea, the faster *Fitzgerald* had overtaken the *Anderson* and was now in the lead as the two ships sailed into somewhat calmer conditions near the eye of one of the fiercest November storms ever recorded on Lake Superior. At about 8 a.m., the *Fitzgerald* was approximately 20 miles south-southwest of the Battle Island Light that marks the entry to Nipigon Bay and turned from its northeasterly heading to travel directly east for a couple of hours, which would take them to a point about 10 miles south of the Slate Islands, where they would again change headings to commence the south-southeast leg of the route. The slower *Anderson* was able to maintain a relative position to the *Fitzgerald* by taking shortcuts through the turns, although the *Fitz* did stretch its lead to some 10 to 15 miles through the morning and early afternoon hours.

Once Captain Paquette's *Wilfred Sykes* was sheltered behind the Sleeping Giant in Thunder Bay, they dropped anchor at 0830 on November 10 and the captain began planning their next move, but First Mate Carlson now called his attention to the barometer.

"The reading, 28.56 inches, was the lowest either of us had ever seen and we made note of it in the log, while agreeing there was little wonder that this storm was so violent. We also concluded that it would prove to be one of the famous 100-year storms, which it did, obviously."

Meteorologists say that barometric readings from about 29.85 to 30.20 inches of mercury are "about normal," with numbers that are lower or higher being classified as low and high pressure areas. Typical low pressure under hurricane conditions runs about 29.1 inches, making the *Sykes'* reading in Thunder Bay unusually low.

Believing that the northeastern winds gathering fury across the full expanse of the lake would be the worst of the storm on the western side of Lake Superior, Paquette also knew that substantial winds would blow in a counterclockwise rotating pattern to the north, then the northwest and west as the front passed out of the Lake Superior area, but the depth of the barometric readings meant those winds would be stronger than he had calculated. Still, he busied himself charting a course to take the *Sykes* into the channel between Isle Royale and Passage Island as the wind came around from the northwest. There, he would be able to study the seas and weather conditions and judge how much the northwest wind might calm the raging northeasterly waves of the night before.

With this plan of action charted, the captain passed the word to the mate on watch that he wanted to be called as the wind came around from the north. He then went below to his quarters, where peace and quiet awaited him – neither of which had been present through those long wild hours of darkness. Laying down, he realized that he hadn't slept in more than 30 hours.

In the calm of his cabin, Paquette thought about the storm they'd just plowed through and his mind drifted to the *Anderson* and *Fitzgerald*, which were still exposed to the wind and waves on the northern reaches of the lake. If they chose to continue sailing, rather than taking shelter at the Slate Islands, they would find almost no protection as they began the southerly leg of that voyage. They'd be sailing with seas coming at them from their starboard rear quarter, again gaining fury across the entire expanse of the lake and continuing to give them navigational problems.

Again he shook his head at their decision not to hug the north shore on their voyage out of Superior, Wisconsin – but they were the masters of their ships, just as he was captain of the *Sykes*. Each of them had the responsibility to make the best decision they were capable of making, but he took some satisfaction in the fact that his prediction of this storm's severity was proving true and that the cautious route he'd chosen had given the ship the easiest trip possible.

He reviewed his own plan to sail to Passage Island and look over the seas from that vantage point. He expected that when the winds switched to the northwest they would knock down the seas relatively quickly. If that proved to be the case, the northwest winds would produce a period of relatively smooth sailing before a following sea developed that would literally push the *Sykes* on its southeast heading toward Whitefish Bay and Sault Ste. Marie. If the seas weren't to his liking at Passage, he could turn around and return to Thunder Bay or hide in the lee off the southeasterly shore of Isle Royale. Having reviewed every aspect of his plan and satisfied himself with the details, Paquette dropped into dreamless sleep.

Asked what he meant at the end of that fateful voyage when he told the owner company's attorneys he felt negligence was the cause of the *Fitzgerald* sinking, Paquette says, "What else could I say? I was listening on the radio when those two captains decided to ignore the weather advisories that I'd been monitoring during a good part of my trip from Indiana Harbor (Indiana) to Superior the day before the storm built up during the night of November 9 and 10.

"I don't think either of them would have ignored the forecast, if they were on their own, but they were running together in beautiful weather that afternoon. As a captain, I know that they didn't want to lose the time it would take to sail the longer, more sheltered route that I took on the north shore because every captain feels pressure from the fleet office to keep to their schedule and avoid the cost of a longer route.

"Plain and simple, they doubted the weather forecasts and talked one another into taking the regular shipping lane. I listened to them talk on the radio about the forecast and finally agree to stick to the regular shipping lane, sailing into the open lake and right into the leading edge of that storm front."

He pauses, then continues, "Those lawyers that I talked to didn't want to hear anything about negligence. They left my boat in a helluva hurry and nobody ever called me to testify during the hearings – even though I was one of only three or four masters who sailed in the worst of that storm."

But the confidence to simply and bluntly state his opinion about the wreck was not gained without a long apprenticeship in the company of a wide variety of seagoing characters – many of whom he found it necessary to confront head-on – and was based on the same experience and judgment that led him to take the more protected route near the Minnesota and Ontario north shore. By this point in his career, Captain Paquette's history of sailing stretched back 32 years, including civilian service on the Atlantic Ocean in World War II and several years of seagoing experience at a time of life that would normally be thought of as school days.

Indeed, at the end of his sophomore year of high school in the spring of 1943, young Dud Paquette figured it was time he started to earn his keep.

"I was big for my age and all of the hockey that I played meant I was in good shape and fairly tough for just being a punk kid," he says. "I was too young to drive, so I rode my bicycle down to the ore docks in Marquette and hung around until the captain of the old SS *Chacornac* came ashore and I asked him for a job."

The captain, decked out in the full regalia of his rating, looked the husky boy over and pointed to the cables tying the ship to the dock. "Do you think you can handle those lines?"

Dud studied them a moment, saying, "I don't think that would be a problem, if that's my job."

The old man nodded and said, "Get your stuff and be aboard in an hour – and be ready to work!"

Captain Paquette's first experience at sea was as a 16-year-old deckhand on the Chacornac, *a former Cleveland Cliffs boat that had previously sailed as the* Cadillac.

Today, Captain Paquette grins and says, "Man, I'll tell you that bicycle flew on the way back to my grandma's house, where I told her I was hired, got my gear and begged my uncle for a ride back to the boat. Grandma didn't like this at all, but Uncle Ray told her I'd never last on the boats, so she let me go. That's how it all started.

"The companies had a helluva time filling crews in World War II, so they didn't ask too many questions and I figured if they believed I was 18, which crewmen were supposed to be, I wasn't going to tell them otherwise."

Thus, a bit shy of his 16th birthday, he became a deckhand aboard a U.S. Maritime Commission wartime ore freighter that had sailed the year before as Cleveland Cliffs' SS *Cadillac*.

"That first trip was iron ore from Marquette to Cleveland, Ohio, where we loaded consumer coal bound for Green Bay, Wisconsin. The first surprise to me was my quarters, which was just a little cubbyhole I shared with another guy. It was so small only one of us could stand up in it at a time. The second surprise was that there was one bathroom for 11 of us deckhands and it was in the steam windlass room for the anchor. It was always 80 or 90 degrees in there, so you didn't take long to do what you had to do and get out.

"When we got to Cleveland, I got another surprise because they put us into the hold to sweep every bit of ore into the shuttles, so none was wasted. Then we had to wash down the entire hold before the coal was loaded, so iron ore didn't contaminate the coal."

He laughs. "Loading the coal was going to take about 36-hours and some of the older crewmen decided that two of us young guys making our first trip needed to get to know about life up the street. The place they took us was really fancy, with a nice bar and elaborate decoration, and I went upstairs with a redheaded lady. I was gone quite awhile and their bar bill must have gotten pretty big because they came looking for me and dragged me back to the ship."

He also remembers the ship as being somewhat less cushy than its automotive namesake from the previous season. "I almost got fired when the cook caught me stealing a glass of milk," he laughs. "In those days the crew only got enough milk to put on their cereal. I was still growing and really liked milk, so I snuck a few glasses before I got caught.

"The old man raised holy hell with me, but he didn't throw me off the boat, so I was able to keep sailing. I was probably just lucky that they needed everybody they could hire."

While noting that pilfering milk could get a sailor fired, he says there was definitely a double standard for officers. Any fruit that came aboard the ship went to the captain's table where the officers ate and the same was true of the cream that was skimmed from the top of the unhomogenized milk that was delivered to the boats in five gallon cans.

"It didn't take me long to decide I'd rather be an officer, if I was going to continue sailing," he says.

"Sailing was a lot different in those days. We knew that we were doing a job that was critical to the war effort, so we felt important. The money was nothing like today, of course, but it was okay, and you got to spend time in the cities you tied up in, because loading and, especially, unloading took a lot longer than it does today. Nowadays, with modern docks and self-unloading equipment on the ships, there's barely time to get a haircut while you're tied up in port."

A big boy who was rapidly proving his manhood, with confidence in his own ability, Paquette says, "A lot of the old-time sailors didn't care if they moved up to higher ratings. They were happy to work, hit the saloons and visit the ladies of the evening in port, and have their winters off."

The remainder of that first season was pretty well routine, with iron ore cargoes downbound from Escanaba, Michigan, to Cleveland, and hard eastern coal upbound to heat homes and fire the boilers that supplied steam for nearly all of the equipment used in the mines and other heavy work. One vivid memory remains from his second trip, however, when the *Chacornac* hauled coal into Munising, Michigan. "It took a day or more to unload, so another guy and I went into town. We were walking around looking at the town and I remember seeing a sign on one business that was funny, but kind of sad too. It said, 'No CCC boys or dogs allowed.' A lot of those CCC (Civilian Conservation Corps, a Depression work program for young men) boys were already in the service and off to war."

After six months as a deckhand, he earned his able seaman's (AB) ticket, though barely 16 years of age. An AB qualified for wheelman, watchman and deck watch duties, worked four hours on with eight off and earned slightly better money than deckhands. They also worked from the pilothouse, in close contact with the captain and mates.

With accreditation as an AB, he boarded the SS *Marquette* at the start of the 1944 season, looking forward to the new season and the new responsibilities at the wheel and on watch. But fate had a different plan for that year – and more.

"We went to Cleveland for coal. A friend and I actually went to an ice cream parlor, believe it or not, and then called a couple of girls we knew to go to a movie."

At the home of one of the girls, a quarantine notice was posted. "The poster said the quarantine was for chicken pox and I knew I'd had it and was immune, so I went in and the man inside was just covered by pox.

"I wasn't worried because I was immune and we went to the movie, then back to the boat and got under way for Green Bay to unload the coal. By the time we were leaving Green Bay, I felt bad and passed out on the trip up to Escanaba. The crew threw me in my bunk and the cook mixed up some concoction out of whiskey and gave it to me."

The doctor at the Public Health Service office insisted he had chicken pox despite Paquette's insistence that he'd had it as a child and couldn't get it again.

"In the hospital, a retired Public Health Service doctor who stopped in to visit finally took a look at me and said that I had small pox – a much more serious disease," he says. "They put me in isolation and issued orders that anybody that I'd had contact with had to be inoculated, from elevator operators to the crew on the boat – everybody. It must have been rare in those days to see small pox, because it seemed like every doctor and nurse in the area came in to have a look at me."

In addition to inoculation, the crewmen were sent home or were boarded at hotels, the ship was completely shuttered and fumigated and a week or more of sailing time was lost.

"As I started feeling better, I got kind of worried about what the company would do to me, but they were okay about it," he says. "I just didn't feel like going back aboard and facing all the guff that I knew I'd get from the crew, so I took a little time off and then called the War Shipping Administration (WSA) office in Cleveland to see what they had to offer."

What they had was an assignment at Norfolk, Virginia, as an AB aboard the SS *Robert Newell,* a North Atlantic freighter being loaded with ammunition, lard, bales of tobacco, peas and other general cargo.

He remembers, "We sailed from Norfolk up to New York City, where we loaded tanks and trucks on the deck and then joined a convoy of about 120 ships bound for England.

"It was late in the year and that was really a slow boat. We only had a top speed of maybe 10 knots and the convoy could only travel as fast as the slowest boats. We were sailing zigzags to keep the German U-boats from having an easy time tracking us, so the trip took 16 or 18 days, but we still lost something like 23 of the ships we sailed with to the enemy or weather."

He remembers that the bridge on the *Newell* had nothing but a canvas tarp overhead. It was often frigid during the three-hour shifts that were equally divided 1.5 hours of wheeling and 1.5 hours on lookout. Captain Mass was 80 years old and Paquette remembers standing watch on the wing of the bridge one particularly nasty day when the old man came up, patted his arm and said, "Let this be a lesson to you, young man. When you get back to the States, never set foot on a ship again."

He laughs and says, "I think I'm lucky that I didn't take his advice."

But Paquette also remembers how miserable that slow boat was when he stood lookout watch. While the bridge was crude, this duty station was positively primitive – just an iron cubicle welded to a top of the king post, with nothing more than a sling to sit on. As waves rolled the boat, this precarious perch swung so far over to the side that a fall would have plunged him directly into the sea.

"We unloaded part of the cargo in England and then sailed down to Cardiff, Wales, to unload the rest, using our deck equipment to place everything on barges, which then took the cargo ashore. We were there a month, so we had time on the beach and I did get to go into London and had a room at one of the better hotels there. One funny thing I remember from that trip was that the ladies of the evening in Cardiff were saltier than any of the sailors, but when they saw that we weren't buying what they were selling, they begged us to get them nylon stockings and, of all things, American playing cards. We never did figure out why they especially wanted American playing cards or what difference it made."

Looking back on his days as an AB, he says, "Wheeling, or steering, was my first chance to really feel the boat and I think that's when I figured out that a good ship handler needs to be aware of how his ship is reacting to the situation he's in. A good touch is partly instinct and partly experience, but without it a captain can get into real trouble – even with the best ship in the world."

Back in the United States, after a 26-day voyage through rough seas dodging German submarines, he landed at Boston, went home for Christmas and then took reassignment from the WSA on the SS *Cristoble,* a ship built in 1940 for commerce in the Caribbean that had been converted into a troop ship. It was faster than his first wartime ship, making the round trip to England in 28 days, unloading troops in Scotland and several other locations in Great Britain.

"Even though Great Lakes sailors were highly respected as wheelmen, my next assignment was quartermaster aboard the SS *Wauhatchie,* a new T-2 tanker that would make 17 knots an hour and could stay with a fast convoy. Former presidential candidate Wendell Wilkie's son was commander of our ship and may have even been in charge of the whole convoy. We sailed with more than 100,000 barrels of high test aviation fuel heading for Cherbourg, France, where the invasion of Europe was under way."

At their destination, they discovered that dive bombers had destroyed the end of the dock where they would normally have unloaded, so they used a makeshift wooden structure for that task. On their return from that 1945 trip, he remembers going with some shipmates to the Hurricane Club on Times Square in New York City, where Ted Lewis and his band were performing, then walking on top of a crowd of taxis at the end of the night. Obviously, police soon ended their stroll over the hoods of cabs, taking them back to their ship. But his big surprise at the end of this trip greeted him when he returned to his hometown, for he was now 18 years old and eligible for the draft – indeed he was drafted.

"I was kind of surprised to get called for the draft, because the war was over and I was working in a job that I thought was important. I figured the draft board in Marquette would exempt me, but they didn't and I reported to Milwaukee with hundreds of other guys. I had been warned to take all my sailing documents as proof that I had experience at sea and I was lucky I did, because out of all those guys who were called, only about six of us ended up going into the Navy. The rest were all drafted into the Army."

He spent a year on active duty as a Naval reservist, but the Navy wasn't really interested in active duty reservists at that point and he was discharged in July 1946 at Bremerton, Washington.

During his tour in the Navy, however, he married his first wife, Leone, a hometown girl from Marquette who accompanied him to Bremerton when he was transferred there from Great Lakes Naval Training Center in Chicago. He also completed his high school diploma in Bremerton and enrolled at the University of Washington in Seattle.

"In some ways, we were lucky to be in the Navy at the time because Leone had juvenile diabetes and almost died during the pregnancy and delivery of our son, Gary," he says. "Those service doctors did one helluva job just to save her and the baby, but she was so sick that we went back to Marquette after my discharge, so she could be near her family."

Back home, Leone remained in poor health and he was unsure of his next step. With a sick wife, a child, still less than 20 years of age and eligible for GI Bill educational benefits, he thought of enrolling in law school at Marquette University, but, with tens of thousands of returning World War II vets entering college level schools, he was told his best bet was to enroll in a two-year college about two hours south of Marquette in Escanaba.

"I guess you'd call it a junior college today," he says. "But the classes went on year-round and the two-year accounting degree took me about 13 months. We had $90 a month coming in from the GI Bill, I made $75 a month playing semi-pro hockey for the Escanaba Hawks during the winter and I also worked at an auto dealership in town that paid me $50 to keep their books because I was playing hockey and they helped sponsor the team."

With the help of his in-laws, they obtained a home in Escanaba and Leone's mother, Edith Levine, moved in to help with the baby, the household chores and Leone's illness.

After obtaining his college degree, he held a job in a Certified Public Accounting office in Escanaba for about a year, but Leone remained in ill health and her medical bills and the low pay he received didn't allow him to get ahead.

36

"One day I looked out and a boat from the Interlake Steamship Company was at the dock in Escanaba," he remembers. "A friend of mine from the Hawks hockey team was a crewman on the boat and I met him to shoot the breeze when he came ashore. He told me I should think about going back to sailing, since I had my AB and a few years on boats. He also said the pay and working conditions on Great Lakes boats were a lot better than when I first sailed."

Paquette thought about it and decided that it made sense, given his family and financial situation. He applied, was hired and went wheeling on the SS *Arcturus* in 1949.

"I'll never forget that the old man, Captain John B. Madigan from Buffalo, New York, told me that I should go to the Lake Carriers' Association navigation school and get a mate's rating."

Although the requirement to apply for navigation school was 36 months of accredited AB service, the shorter Great Lakes season was counted as a full 12 months and even those standards were relaxed somewhat in the war years. So, by the time he had actually turned 18 in 1945 and his local draft board tapped him for service, he was close to fulfilling the requirements to enter navigation school that would qualify him for a mate's rating.

"When I checked my records, I needed three months at the wheel to qualify. At tie-up that fall, I had three months and one day of wheeling, so I applied, was accepted and finished school in time for the 1950 season."

Conducted in Cleveland, Ohio, the Lake Carriers' Association classes were instructed by working masters from several fleets, who taught the latest in navigational and meteorological techniques to the dozens of candidates for mate ratings each year.

Upon graduating, he had job offers as mate with several fleets, but did a bit of research and found that a ship he particularly admired, the recently launched 678-foot SS *Wilfred Sykes,* belonged to the Inland Steel Company fleet. The company was hiring mates. He hired on as a third mate and was assigned to the old SS *Joseph Block,* starting a 30-year career as an officer with that fleet.

"I was only a 22-year-old kid when I got my mate's license and had no seniority as an officer, but the shipping tonnages were really high in those days – way over 60 million tons a season, as I recall – and even the biggest boats only hauled a little more than 20,000 tons, so there were a lot of boats and jobs for all of us that held ratings.

"In my career, I served as mate and master of every one of Inland Steel's boats, but I guess it's no secret that I always thought the *Sykes* was special," Paquette says. "It was the supership of the

Great Lakes when it came out in 1949, even though a lot of people called it a white elephant, saying it was so long it would never be able to maneuver in ports and predicting all sorts of other problems. It wasn't as big or as powerful as the boats that came out later, but I always thought it was a great boat and I'm glad it was the boat I was on in the storm that sank the *Fitzgerald*.

"We took some huge seas over our bow in the early part of the storm and over our stern and weather deck as the wind rotated around to the northwest after we left Thunder Bay on November 10. She was rockin' and rollin' for practically the whole two days of that storm, but she never missed a beat on that whole trip."

CHAPTER THREE

Mastering the Craft

By noon on November 10, 1975, having slept a couple of hours, Captain Dudley Paquette was back on the bridge reviewing the charted weather information. Current information mapped by the mates showed that his expectation that the wind would come around counterclockwise was being met, as the wind had steadily rotated from north-northeast to north and kept coming around. In the shelter of Thunder Bay, they again made a complete check of all hatches and other water-tight points, then weighed anchor and made way out of Thunder Bay at 1245 hours.

"My plan only covered the 25 miles or so to Passage Island, because I wanted to have the option to turn back and again take shelter if I didn't like what I saw when we got to the open lake."

Once they reached Passage Island, he was able to confirm his prediction that the northeast seas would subside in the onslaught of northwesterly winds, which had now kicked up to 40-50 knots from 290 degrees, the northwester he had expected. If he decided to continue, they would be sailing with a trailing sea.

As he surveyed the seas, the radio came to life. "Inland vessel off Passage Island, this is the *Roger Blough*. Over."

Paquette's ears perked up at the welcome voice of Captain Neal Rolfson, who had been one of his instructors and earned his respect years before in navigation school. At 858 feet with a beam of 105 feet, the *Blough* was the biggest ore carrier in the U.S. Steel Corporation fleet and had been launched just three years earlier.

"*Blough* this is the *Wilfred Sykes*. Is that you, Neal?"

The radio crackled back, "Roger, Dudley. Were you out in the blow?"

"Most of it. We stayed on the north shore and dropped anchor in Thunder Bay a few hours this morning, but this is quite a storm. What about you?"

"Yeah, we're hove-to off Rock Harbor (Isle Royale), but it didn't give us much shelter, so we took a beating. What's happening with these northeast seas?"

"The northeast is subsiding and the wind is coming around to the northwest. We don't have to worry any more about a northeast sea," Paquette said. "I figure in an hour or two we'll be in following seas and I'm planning to run for Whitefish (Point and Bay, at the southeastern corner of Lake Superior)."

Rolfson paused a moment, then came back, "Well, you're the weatherman, Dudley, so you must have it figured out. I'll fall in behind you and follow you down."

"Okay, Neal – good to have you with us."

As the conversation ended about 3:45 p.m., Captain Paquette rang full ahead on the Chadburn telegraph to the engine room and laid a pair of triangles on the pilothouse chart, plotting a 120 degree, straight line route bisecting the heart of Lake Superior from Passage Island to Whitefish Point. Trusting his weather knowledge, but knowing the seas would pile up behind them, Captain Paquette says he wanted to get some miles behind him before the heavier seas developed, but the backside of this storm would prove to last longer and blow stronger than even his prediction had calculated.

Thus was he committed to a voyage that would become a major memory from his 32-year sailing career, as well as a piece of the legend of the sinking of the *Edmund Fitzgerald*.

But why would he make the decision to leave the relative security of Thunder Bay and proceed down the lake, knowing the seas would build in the face of strong winds blowing at his stern?

Captain Riley Ward, an officer and master for 35 years with the Inland Fleet, served with Paquette aboard several vessels and says it would have been no surprise to his crew that this captain chose to leave Thunder Bay with a storm in progress.

"Dudley didn't very often lay up for weather and he really didn't like to hang on an anchor," Ward says. "He was pretty much a heavy-weather captain, but he'd always tell us, 'Don't worry boys, I've got us the smoothest ride possible.'"

Saying that Paquette had the best judgment of anyone he ever sailed with, Captain Ward adds, "He was way ahead of everybody else when it came to forecasting weather. Nowadays, with all of the electronic equipment on ships, we get regular weather maps printed out right in our chart room, but Dudley had us mates record all the Weather Service information and draw in the isobars on the plastic cover of a weather chart that we kept updated at all times. It was a real pain for his mates – but he could almost always predict what the weather was going to be way before the Weather Service and he did figure out ways to make the run as comfortable as possible."

* * *

These skills were honed by years of experience in every conceivable weather situation as a deckhand and AB, in classes on the most modern instrumentation during navigation school and at manufacturers' classes, as well as watch duty as a mate under a wide variety of masters from the Inland fleet.

With his brand new mate's rating, 22-year-old Dudley Paquette reported at the start of the 1950 season for duty as third mate on Inland Steel's old SS *Joseph Block*, a 2,000-horsepower ship built in 1906 that was commonly the first assignment for new officers of the Inland Fleet.

During his time as an able seaman (AB), he had observed that there were subtleties that separated the men who mastered ships from those who remained in AB ratings or were content to spend their time standing watch as mates. In his new position, he set out to understand those differences under the command of Captain Sidney J. Ward, a master he would serve with a couple of times through the years and one of the classic, old-time breed of captain.

"The day before we were scheduled to depart, I went aboard at Indiana Harbor," he remembers. "The cook's name was McDonald and he was a tough one. He told me my mates' quarters up front weren't ready, but I could bunk aft in the crew's area for the night. I got set up there and walked up to have a look at my quarters in the front of the boat, only to find that it wasn't much bigger than what I'd had as a deckhand on the old *Chacornac*. When I said something to Mac about it, he growled, 'What the hell do you think this is, the Waldorf-Astoria?'"

Just the first of many crusty characters – especially cooks – that Paquette would meet during his days as a fleet officer, this cook is particularly memorable to Paquette because he was always shocked by Mac's treatment of his wife, Gladys Birdie, who was also on the galley staff.

"Every time his wife would do something he didn't like, he'd cuss her out and kick her in the legs," Paquette remembers. "You should have seen the shape those legs were in.

"It seemed like most of the cooks I met were tough and cranky. It was common in those days for their wives to work with them and a lot of them abused their wives in one way or another when they worked together."

This first assignment also taught him that his earlier observation aboard the *Chacornac* was still true. As an officer, he now had free access to milk when he wanted it, and rank had other privileges as well.

"The best cut of meat was served to the senior officer," he says, remembering that one evening he was the first officer to enter the officers' dining room and Gladys Birdie hollered into the kitchen that the first mate had just come in for dinner.

"Old Mac gave me the First Mate's steak and I dug right in," he chuckles. "A minute or two later, Gladys Birdie told Mac that she needed dinner for the Chief Mate. Old Mac yelled and hollered, called her every name in the books and kicked her in the legs, but I had already started, so I got his steak and the First had to settle for the next best cut that night."

Booze was a continual source of trouble. "The sailors found all kinds of ways to get booze aboard," he admits. "That first season, we knew some of them were smuggling it onto the ship and I finally caught them. They used the gangway at the fantail and would throw the booze through the open engine room door to a guy inside. Once we figured that out, we put a stop to it."

He also remembers that many captains at that time were reluctant to allow their mates to polish their skills with new equipment such as radar – which was a relatively new addition to pilothouses of Great Lakes freighters at that time.

"Those old-timers like Captain Ward wanted to save the radar for when they needed it," he explains. "Then, when they could have used the radar, nobody really knew much about it and couldn't recognize what they were seeing or didn't trust what the radar was showing them. That's why I had my mates working the radars all the time after I made captain. I knew what radar could do because I'd been to some pretty tough classes, and I wanted my officers to know what they were looking at and believe what the radar showed."

But Paquette's most vivid memory of his first season as a mate is the late November loading of wet ore at Marquette.

"We had taken on a list and were in the trough of the seas when I got out on deck, still pulling on my life jacket as I went. There was (First Mate) Tom Olson, sucking on his cigarette and

As a new third mate on the old SS Joseph Block, Dudley Paquette set out to learn what the seas and seasoned captains could teach him. Among the thornier issues he encountered were tough, cranky cooks.

tapping on the dial of the Draft-O-Meter like he didn't believe it. We finally got the ship to come around, headed back into the harbor and tied up.

"We were pumping water out of that sloppy cargo for so long that the company started to make plans to lay the ship up in Marquette," he says. "They told me that I would be assigned as winter ship watcher, since Marquette was my hometown. I had other plans and I was sure the hell glad when we got a spell of nice weather and were able to get down to Indiana Harbor, unload that ore and lay the ship up there, where somebody else could watch her."

Although he lacked the seniority that would be needed to hold a mate's position today, he went back on the *Joseph Block* in 1951 as third mate, then was transferred in June at the same rating to the flagship of the Inland Fleet, the SS *Wilfred Sykes,* the ship he had admired so much that it led to his joining the Inland fleet.

"George W. Fisher was captain and the *Sykes* was just the Queen of Sheba on the Great Lakes at the time – a big, beautiful boat that drew crowds wherever we went. We had all the officials and important guests of the company riding with us, and it didn't take me long to figure out that a captain not only had to be a good ship handler, he also had to be good at handling himself around guests that had the power to make or break his career or the career of anybody on the crew.

43

"Anyway, getting back to the *Sykes*, I really believe the Army Corps of Engineers deliberately scheduled us through the MacArthur Lock every time we'd lock through the Soo, because that was the closest lock to the viewing area and there was always a crowd to gawk at us as we passed."

Captain Fisher was a particularly important influence in Paquette's career and one of the grand old men of Great Lakes shipping. Born in Rumania, Fisher came to Canada and worked in shipyards there before taking a job with American Ship, being promoted to positions there and with Hutchinson & Co., a transportation company that managed the Inland Fleet. He was assigned to the master's position on the *Wilfred Sykes* after the first captain died.

"Captain Fisher was a master ship handler," Dudley assesses his mentor. "He also held the power of life and death on his boat. He could just wave his hand and you'd be gone, but he always seemed to like me."

With a thick accent, Fisher found Paquette's first name troublesome and "Dud" became "Dot" to the Old Man. One day, he called Dudley aside in the pilothouse and said, "Dot, dat damned Gallagher says he wants off in Duluth-Superior (their next port). Find out why he wants to leave after only a few days on boat."

Not really concerned with the loss of a seaman, but knowing the old man wasn't fooling around, Dudley reluctantly agreed to pry into Bob Gallagher's reasoning.

"I was going back to the galley and Gallagher was just ahead of me, so I stopped him and told him that the Old Man had asked me to find out why he was quitting such a nice boat after only a few days. After all, every seaman seemed to want to serve on the *Sykes* in those days."

Gallagher thought a moment, grinned and said, "Well, Mate, you tell the Old Man that it's just too damned far to walk back to breakfast."

Dudley laughs and says, "You should have heard old Fisher yelling. 'That damned no-good SOB' was just the start of it, but Gallagher left the boat in Duluth and we laughed about it later because the 500 feet or so from the pilothouse to the galley did seem like a long walk in those days."

He also remembers that the cook's name was Lawrence Green and that Olive, his wife, also served in the galley of the *Sykes*. Green was another of the tough old cooks that seemed to dog him

Guests got VIP treatment on ore boats, many of which had special accommodations for entertaining company officials, customers, friends and investors. This is the guest lounge on the Wilfred Sykes.

wherever he was assigned. At any rate, the crew complained bitterly about the gravy, after one of the watchmen saw Green cutting a pound of lard into the gravy pot and stirring in that fat to eke more life from the tasty drippings of roasts and other meats.

"I mentioned to the watchman who caught Green that if I were him, that gravy pot would disappear," Dudley laughs. "It wasn't long after that that the pot was gone and Green was hollering and yelling that the gravy pot was expensive stainless steel and company property – but there wasn't anything he could do, other than raise hell.

"Our last trip of the 1951 season was into Duluth-Superior for frozen ore, so we were there about a week in the downtown area. Even with the cold weather at that time of year, we still had big crowds come out to look at the ship – that's how special it was."

Back as third mate on the *Sykes* at the April 3 start of the 1952 season, Dudley remembers this as the year that he first stepped up temporarily to second mate. He also remembers an evening early in the season when Captain Fisher was trying to get stock market news.

"He loved to play the market and was always calling his broker on the radio phone. He was upset with the market at the time but, before he was able to find the evening stock market report on the radio, he had to go back and eat with the guests we had aboard, so he told me to listen up while he was gone.

"We were out at sea and I couldn't get anything but static and baseball on the radio while he was gone. When he came back, I told him I hadn't been able to find a market report and he began to fiddle with the dial, changing stations, getting baseball games on every station that came in, and he started swearing. Finally, he banged his hand on the table and I couldn't keep a straight face when he yelled, 'God dammit to hell! All I hear is high balls, low balls, blue balls and red balls and no damned stock prices.'"

The old man was also an avid newspaper reader – but only the serious stuff. He always threw the comics section away.

"I'd dig out the funny papers and read them. One time, I looked up and the old man was watching me read the funny papers and asked, 'Dot, who dis Dick Tracy fellow, anyway?'

"No matter how I tried, I just couldn't make him understand Dick Tracy – but he was sure a master at handling a ship, and I was fortunate to serve under him those two seasons before I applied for masters school at the end of the 1952 season."

During that season, he remembers another situation when he was able to aggravate Green the cook. One hot afternoon in Duluth-Superior, he decided to give the deckhands some ice cream bars from the galley's freezer. Since the freezer was located on the open deck outside the galley, it was easily accessible and, with his first raid a success, he repeated his pilferage at other times when the weather made ice cream a treat.

"When Green discovered that the ice cream was missing, he demanded that the first mate have a lock installed on the reefer, which the chief had me do. He even had me solder the screws, so he was sure nobody could take the hasps off. A few days later, I decided to give the boys ice cream again, but I wanted Green to know I'd been in his freezer, so I knocked a few things over and made a mess inside.

"Later, the first and the chief engineer were back at the fantail talking and I joined them.

"'Mate,' the first says to me. 'Green tells me somebody's been in his freezer again. How did you do that?'

"I laughed and told him, 'He forgot that locks always come with two keys. I gave Green one of them, but kept the second one.'

"The first just laughed and told me I'd better watch out that Green didn't take a cleaver to me."

At the end of the 1952 season, Dudley had completed the Coast Guard requirement of three years' service as a licensed mate on a first class vessel and was accepted into the January 1953 Lake

Carriers' Association navigation school to qualify for his master's certificate.

"I had studied the better part of the previous summer and didn't have any real trouble with the classwork, but they used Coast Guard guys to grade some of the papers and this one SOB thought I was too young to be a master. In fact, he told me, 'There are a lot of older officers that deserve to be masters before you. It'll be 20 years before you get a captain's spot, so why are you wasting our time like this?'

"One of the last exercises in the class was to make up a fake accident and do all the proper paperwork for it. I did mine and sent the papers in, but they came back disapproved. I redid them, sent them in again and that damned Coast Guardsman sent them back. This went on until damned near the start of the season. Finally, I got in touch with old Captain John Murray, who was head of the school and an apostle of the U.S. Steel Fleet, and he told me just to send my papers to him and he'd see I got my license. I sent them in to Captain Murray, he took care of it and I never heard another word from that damned Coast Guardsman."

After receiving his master's license, he was promoted to second mate and again assigned to the old *Joseph Block* for the start of the 1953 season.

"I reported aboard, proud as punch of my new master's ticket, but the first mate didn't have his master's rating and that didn't go down so good. Luckily, I was big enough to handle myself."

During that first season as a second mate, Dudley discovered that the second's normal midnight to 4 a.m. watch was one of the more interesting shifts a mate can stand.

"When we were in port, that was the shift when the boys would come back to the ship and they'd usually be real well organized, after spending the night in the saloons," he says. "I lifted the front ladder just out of reach, because I didn't want any of them getting hurt by trying to use it when they weren't capable. You should have heard the hell they raised about that 'damned mate' worrying so much."

He also shook down the crew for any booze they might try to smuggle aboard, although he admits he'd overlook the occasional six-pack of beer, if the crewman didn't abuse that oversight.

"In May of that year, we left downbound from Superior and ran into a helluva northeaster," he says. "The first rousted me out of bed to help shutter the pilothouse windows and we were lucky that we did because we took waves over the bow that actually buckled the bulwarks on our Texas deck (the deck below the pilothouse) and bent the overhang and the stringers over the lounge and did other damage to the front of the boat.

"We reduced rpms so we had just enough power to steer her, took shelter off Devils Island in the Apostles and spent the night there. That's where we heard about the *Steinbrenner* sinking off Isle Royale. We talked with Captain Fisher on the *Sykes* the next day and he told us that they had been involved in the rescue efforts and actually launched one of their lifeboats to help in the rescue."

He pauses, then says, "After that storm, we found that the pump on our Number 3 hold sucked out some iron-colored water and we wondered what had happened. The ship had been remodeled and was fitted with modern patent hatch covers, even though it had been built in 1906, and we had never had water get into the hold before. We never did figure out if water leaked in or if it had rained just before or during the time we were loading – but I always figured it rained. Still, I did think about that after the Coast Guard blamed the hatch covers for the sinking of the *Fitzgerald*."

The fall of that season, the *Maryland* was blown ashore between Grand Island and Marquette during a September storm.

"We were hove-to off Caribou Island, waiting for the wind to subside before going into Marquette Harbor and heard the whole thing on the radio. I don't remember if they had engine trouble or lost their helm, but we sailed by after the ship was on the beach and what a sight – high and dry and just sitting up there. Even the rudder was out of the water. I remember that it took a week or more for tugs to pull it off the beach and refloat it."

On the personal side of the 1953 sailing season, his wife, Leone, who had never really been in good health, died of the juvenile diabetes from which she suffered. His Grandmother Paquette cared for their son, Gary, until Dudley remarried, when his wife, Mary, assumed that responsibility and, during the long months he was at sea, most other parenting duties for the three children they had together.

In the 1954 and 1955 seasons, he reported as second mate on the *Wilfred Sykes*, re-joining his old friend, Captain Fisher.

"I guess Captain Fisher must have liked me, because he could have any mate he wanted and I was assigned with him," Dudley says. "I heard that he told Carl Jacobs, the Inland vice president of raw materials, that I was a good man, but I had a sharp tongue."

He chuckles and says, "I think the reason he said that is because I was standing by one time when we were tying up. The first mate was at the railing calling our distances from the dock over the intercom – '12 feet, 10 feet, 8 feet,' and so on. He forgot to flip off the intercom and I yelled, 'Slam! Bang! Right against it!' The first almost died when he saw that the speaker was on and realized the Old Man might think it was him talking.

"I let him stew for a while and then confessed to Captain Fisher that it was me he heard on the intercom, so that's probably why he figured that I had a sharp tongue."

The 1954 season saw shipments of iron ore drop by 36 million tons from the previous year and proved to be the beginning of a long period of fluctuating, cyclical demand for steel and, consequently, for iron ore. This fluctuating demand cycle would continue through three decades, putting pressures on the steel industry and, in a number of cases, leading to mergers or outright failure of some companies. The following season, tonnages improved, but the rhythm of four hours on and eight off continued uneventfully for the youthful second mate and his shipmates. Their boat still commanded attention wherever it went and there was always a cargo awaiting it at one port or another.

Small things can sometimes mark a season as memorable. Dudley recalls, "The wheelman on my watch smoked cigarettes and was too cheap to buy tailor-mades. He rolled his own and always made a big mess in the pilothouse, with loose tobacco scattered all over. I got tired of it and noticed one day that Green the cook had 15 or 20 cartons of cigarettes stashed away near the galley. I knew that the grocery supplier was smuggling them in wrapped in grocers' paper as a bribe to Green and that Olive, Green's wife, was getting a box of chocolates the same way. It was just common practice for cooks to cheat on the grocery orders in those days and for suppliers to give them bribes, because they weren't paid well and made up for it in their own ways. In fact, many times the captain knew about it and might even be in cahoots with them.

"Anyway, after I found Green's stash of cigarettes, I began to steal a pack of smokes now and then and give them to the wheelman. I kept him in tailor-mades during his watches for the rest of the season. Green had to know, but he never said one word about it and I didn't have to put up with that mess in the pilothouse after that."

In 1956, Dudley boarded the *L.E. Block* in late March and made the acquaintance of Captain William S. Walsh, the self-proclaimed "King of the Toledo Jungle" – who was also known behind his back as "Peaches LaTour."

"He'd walk around on the bridge with his glasses hanging around his neck or pushed down on his nose so he was looking over the top at you and tell anyone who'd listen how tough he was," Dudley chuckles. "I served two seasons with him on that boat and saw how tough he really was when I caught Sulo Heikkinen, the bosun (boatswain), in his bunk stinking drunk when we were tied up and loading. I also found his stash of smuggled booze and was tossing it over the side as I cussed the guy out. He was a real old-timer and big – maybe 6-feet-6 – but he almost had tears in his eyes and was begging, 'Please mate, don't get me thrown off the boat.'

"The Old Man spotted the hullabaloo and came down to see what was going on. After a minute, he told me to just cool down and take it easy. He told me Sulo couldn't give us any serious trouble and that we'd just keep an eye on him until he sobered up. I thought to myself – 'Oh yeah, Cap, you're the King of the Toledo Jungle and some tough guy, all right.'

Another bosun he clearly recalls was Robert Johnson, an old-time sailor who spent virtually all year aboard ships – during the summer performing seagoing crafts and winters as a ship watcher on Inland boats laid up in South Chicago.

"Bobby was a helluva bosun and could do a million things – splice, sew, anything that needed to be done on a ship – but he couldn't leave the booze alone and he really couldn't handle his drinks. I got to like the guy that season, and I took him under my wing and had his drinking down to the point where I could handle him. He eventually got the nickname 'Paquette's Bobby,' because I took care of him.

"I think old Bob knew he had a real problem, because he always sent his paycheck straight home to his wife and she'd cash it and send him back his allowance, which he just couldn't wait to spend in some saloon, once the ship tied up to load or unload. He always came back with a load on and I gave Bobby orders that when he came back on a bender he was to go straight to his bunk, sleep it off and stay off the deck. He always did just that."

A year or two later, when Dudley transferred to the *Ryerson* as first mate, he asked Captain Fisher to request that his Bobby be transferred to the ship and the request was passed along and honored by the fleet office.

"The first time that Captain Fisher ran into my Bobby was in one of the tunnels as the captain was going ashore in Indiana Harbor. Bobby had already been ashore and was stinking drunk, as usual. He was doing what I told him to do, using the tunnel to stay off the deck and get to his bunk to sleep it off.

As second mate on the Sykes, part of Captain Paquette's duties involved the spring inspection by the Coast Guard. Here, he mans the emergency helm with First Mate Bud Johnson, as Captain George W. Fisher, Chief Engineer Al Wolf and the Coast Guard inspector stand by.

"The way Captain Fisher described it, he was bouncing from bulkhead to bulkhead in the tunnel and the captain asked me later, 'Dot, dis fella you bring aboard my ship – you sure he didn't break arm? He shoulda' broke his neck. If I knowed he was a damned drunk, I never let ya take him aboard dis ship!'

"By that time, I knew the captain and I knew he had to have asked for me as his first mate, because he could have any mate he wanted. I told him, 'Cap, Bobby's just like you and me – he likes to drink now and then, but I can handle him and he's a good fella and a helluva worker,' and that was the truth. My Bobby loved the work and the only time he ever got mad at me was when I'd tell him to take it easy.

"Anyway, I took my Bobby with me when I was captain on the old *Joe Block* in 1965 and 1966, because I was really the only one who could handle him. I really felt bad when I heard that Old Bob died in his bunk as a ship watcher on the *Clarence B. Randall* in South Chicago."

But, getting back to Captain Walsh, the King of the Toledo Jungle may have been in a mood to coddle a drunken boatswain, but his attitude was considerably less kindly toward the monkey

51

that his first mate, David Kinnear, brought aboard at the start of the 1956 season.

"Captain Walsh found that critter during inspection, swore a blue streak and the monkey went off that boat in one helluva hurry," Dudley laughs.

"Our 1956 season was shortened quite a bit when the old man hit a big concrete caisson down river in the St. Marys River and did a fair amount of damage to the ship. We ended up in the shipyard from July 7 until well into August. It was a real embarrassment for Captain Walsh, of course."

During the 1957 season on the *L.E. Block*, Dudley alternated as first and second mate, with most of the time as second. He was transferred to the *Philip D. Block* as second mate at the start of the 1958 season, serving under Captain Sidney J. Ward, the old-time captain he'd first served with on the old *Joseph Block* when it nearly turned over in 1950.

"The company expected us to look like officers and to keep the boat shipshape. The old man told me to use my time on watch to clean in the pilothouse," Dudley says. "A day or two later, he came in and I was mopping the floor. He grabbed the mop and threw it overboard, telling me, 'You wipe the floors on my boat on your hands and knees.'

"I got hot and as soon as I could catch him alone, I asked to see him in his office. I told him I'd quit before I'd get on my hands and knees to swab the deck and that I'd go to the company office and tell them exactly why I was quitting. Well, he knew me well enough to know I meant what I said and he backed off and I was good with him after that."

As one of the first boats to undergo a lengthening, the *Philip Block* had also been fitted with patent hatches, a 4,000-horsepower steam engine and a hatch crane, but, as a ship handler, Dudley particularly remembers it as a ship that needed babying.

"They cut the boat in half and added a big section in the middle. It had been 580 feet long and ended up being 672 feet, but, boy, was it limber. You could feel it twist and work up and down, and you knew from the feel that you had to handle it with kid gloves. 'Tender' is what we always called it."

In August, he moved up to first mate, but the big event in his memory of that season was the loss of the *Carl D. Bradley* in a November storm at Boulder Reef in Lake Michigan that was recounted in Chapter One.

Rumors of a steel strike were circulating at the start of the 1959 season, when he reported as second mate on the motor vessel *E.J.*

Block, captained by Thomas A. Olson, who had been the first mate on the old *Joseph Block* when it nearly turned over in the 1950 wet ore episode in Marquette. As usual, Dudley encountered a cook with the temperament of a dictator, as well as a diesel engine that had originally powered a Navy destroyer, but caused the engine room crew endless problems. Those irritants were short-lived, however, as the strike that year by the United Steel Workers of America threatened to close steel plants for prolonged periods.

"I had served as a mate on the company tug and supply boat during a short strike in 1952 and, when the 1959 strike came, I was transferred to Indiana Harbor as captain of the tug that the employees called 'The Strikebreaker,' which was about 50 feet long and had been fitted out as a work boat to carry supplies for the people who were keeping the furnaces going inside the steel mill.

"There were about 1,400 non-union employees that kept the furnaces operating and stayed right in the plant during the strike. We hauled everything they needed into the plant at night – whole truckloads of meat, vegetables, milk, cigarettes and everything else – even prizes for the bingo games they had every night. Every foot of space was used for freight – even the head (toilet) in the pilothouse was used to stow cases of booze so they'd be out of sight.

"The company bought South American ore and barged it up the Mississippi and the canal system from New Orleans to South Chicago. We also got some Canadian ore that was hauled in and unloaded in South Chicago by Canadian self-unloaders. We loaded the ore onto huge barges and moved them by tugs from South Chicago to Indiana Harbor. I think we moved about a half million tons of iron ore through ice that punched several holes in barges and damned near sank one or two of them – but we had to keep the ore going into the plant.

"We'd sleep days and make the supply run every night. That went on for months. One time we were nearly run down by a ship and I'll never forget that the poor guy who was supervisor of the supply operation got seasick almost every trip. We got the stuff where it was needed, though, and there was extra pay in it for us."

He remembers that the strike of 1959 changed forever the relationship of previously non-union ships' officers and the companies.

"When the strike hit, the companies laid off most of the engineers and mates and reduced the captains to half pay to stay aboard and watch their ships," he says. "That didn't affect me directly, of course, because I was on the supply tug, but the companies might just as well have handed all of their officers over to the union, because most of us signed up as members at that time. In fact, when the strike ended, I got a raise in pay that was a third again as much as I'd been making before the union came in."

By the time the strike ended late in 1959, there was little shipping season left, but he returned to the *E.J. Block* and tied up the season December 12 as first mate.

At the start of the 1960 season, he was again assigned as first mate aboard the *E.J. Block,* but that season and the next saw him bouncing around among the Inland ships. The 1960 season was memorable because the *E.J. Block* was damaged when it hit bottom in a turn at Little Rapids Cut of the St. Marys River.

"The boat raised up and almost immediately began taking water," he says. "We managed to make temporary repairs so we could get to Indiana Harbor to unload, then head for the Manitowoc shipyard for repairs. As we were coming in, we met the SS *Edward L. Ryerson* making its trial run. I knew that Captain Fisher was master of the ship and it was fun to get a good look at this brand new flagship of the Inland Fleet on its first trip in open water.

"In those days, the fleet carried a lot of guests for subsidiaries of the company like Ryerson & Co., Inland Steel Container Co. and others. I remember a party of guests from Inland Steel Container that were up from Texas. There was one of the salesmen from our company and five guests, as I remember, and they conned me into a game of gin rummy with them. No matter how I tried to lose, it just seemed like everything I touched turned to gold and I beat their pants off. They couldn't believe I was so lucky and made a point of inviting me down to Texas for a gin rummy party when the season was over – and wouldn't you know that I couldn't lose then either.

"Since the party was all men, we'd get together to tell jokes in the pilothouse and we laughed so hard that nobody could get to sleep at night."

The start of the 1961 season saw him back aboard the *E.J. Block* as second mate and it was on that ship that Dudley met and learned to deal with one of the more memorable characters he was to encounter during his years as a mate. Surprisingly, since, first, this was a *cook* and, second, a *drinker*, Dudley still harbors a bit of a soft spot for Otto Kiesel from Bay City, Michigan, who was hired at the last minute before sailing started.

"Otto couldn't have weighed more than 120 pounds soaking wet and he always seemed to be able to get booze aboard, but just a couple of beers would get him gassed. He was an excellent cook, though, and the crew liked him and didn't want to see him fired, so we put up with the situation.

"Many times, after the first mate relieved me at 1530 (3:30 p.m.), I'd go back and check on him and he'd be passed out in his bunk. That would only be an hour or so before dinner and I'd roust him out, get him on his feet and he'd put out dinner for 30 hungry crewmen – how he did it was a miracle. We couldn't figure out how he was getting his booze aboard and kept checking his grocery orders, but we finally caught him throwing it through the engine room hatchway as he came back aboard the ship."

Dudley bounced back and forth from second to first mate on the ship during the early part of the 1961 season, but the fleet promoted him in mid-June and transferred him as first mate to the *Ryerson,* under Captain Fisher.

"I was glad to be back with this great old captain and to serve on such a classy ship," Dudley says. "And believe me, it was some ship – painted up just like a yacht. We tied up at the Duluth Seaway Terminal for a day during an engineering society meeting there and literally hundreds of people came down to take a tour of the *Ryerson*. A high point of that visit for me was to have Olive Green come aboard. She was the wife of that tough old cook that I stole the ice cream bars from and I couldn't help asking her if they ever figured out who was stealing the ice cream? She laughed and said, 'Dudley, we knew it was you all along.'

"Anyway, as I said earlier, Captain Fisher loved to play the stock market and must have owned stock in a company that built boats or outboard motors or something, because every time we'd pass a recreation boat, he'd grin and say, "Lookit dat, Dot – putt, putt, putt and another 25 cents for me.'"

He returned as first mate under Fisher in 1962 and says, "Our last trip of the season was kind of sad. Captain Fisher was making his last voyage because he'd reached mandatory retirement age of 65 and was the first of three masters who retired that year. At breakfast that last day, he had tears in his eyes. He didn't really want to retire and his wife was a real bearcat, so he didn't have any reason to just stay at home. I felt bad for him, but rules are rules and he had to go."

The following season (1963) as first mate on the *Ryerson,* Dudley remembers a personally pleasing episode in what is now Thunder Bay, Ontario. Company CEO Edward and Mrs. Ryerson were hosting a party of guests so distinguished that they were treated to a tour of the city with the mayor and other dignitaries.

Part of that visit was to include a captain's dinner for the ship's guests and city dignitaries that evening.

"As first mate, I was the deck officer in charge of loading the ship and everything just came together and the loading went perfect. We were really making time. I knew the dock supervisor pretty well and he agreed to keep his crew on overtime to finish loading us.

"It ended up that we loaded the boat in two hours and 16 minutes and were done before the guest party got back from their tour. I told Captain Thomas Olson we were ready to get under way and he damned near blew the cigarette that was always hanging out of his mouth across the pilothouse. He was yelling and hollering like crazy. 'Now you've done it,' he told me. 'What the hell am I gonna tell Mr. Ryerson, with all those dignitaries coming aboard for dinner?'"

Knowing the end of his story, he chuckles and says, "The limos and guests came down the dock for the party and Mr. Ryerson was the first one up the gangplank. Captain Olson met him there and assured him dinner was ready and that we'd delay departure so he could entertain his party.

"Mr. Ryerson, great man that he was, told him, 'Captain, if this ship is loaded, by all means we're going to cancel the dinner party and depart immediately.' The Canadian VIPs were told that we were departing and were escorted off the boat. We left the Thunder Bay breakwater at 1730 (5:30 p.m.) during my watch, so I was on the bridge when Captain Olson had to go back for dinner with the guests. It was part of his duty, but he said that he should send me to take all the grief he figured he was going to get, since I was the one that loaded so fast that it spoiled the party with the Thunder Bay VIPs.

"Evidently at dinner, Captain Olson admitted that I had done a good job, because after dinner, the guests came up on the bridge and Mrs. Ryerson said to me, "You're a smart one, Dudley! Captain Olson says that this is the fastest loading time this ship has ever had and may be one of the fastest for any ship in the fleet.' Later on, when he was thinking of retiring, Tom Olson also told the company that I deserved a chance and could handle the responsibility of my own ship. Since I'd served with him several seasons when he was both a mate and a captain, he knew me real well and I appreciated him putting in a good word for me.

"One night during a bit of a blow, he came up on the bridge and was looking out at the lake. We always got along well and he said, 'Dud, these damned lakes are getting so rough, maybe it's time for me to quit sailing.'

"Later that fall, we were downbound off Manitou Island (off the tip of Keweenaw Peninsula) and ran into a northwest gale in snow and heavy seas. We couldn't do anything with the boat and decided to turn her around into the seas and seek some shelter. We took a wide detour around Superior Shoal and I stayed up there with Captain Olson all night. When things settled down, he shook my hand. As I said before, that's about as close to a compliment or a thank you as officers give each other."

During that winter, Dudley was named "shore captain" in charge of ship watchers and the winter work schedule for the fleet's ships that were laid up in Indiana Harbor and South Chicago. He was also told by the fleet office that he would make captain the next season.

"Being shore captain was some experience, I'll tell you," he laughs. "The ship watchers were required by the insurance company and stayed aboard in the cooks' quarters, which was their winter home. Part of my duty was to be sure the ship watchers were okay and to be sure they didn't have women aboard, for fear that a woman might be involved in an accident that could get us sued. When I'd go aboard, I'd look for heel marks of women's shoes on the gangplank and deck, where there was usually enough snow to see them. When I found heel marks, I'd warn the guy to get the woman off the boat in an hour or I'd raise hell with him.

"The cooks were always the first to report back for fitout and you should have heard the hullabaloo when they'd come back in the spring and start to settle into their quarters – 'There's women's underwear all over the place! What was this guy doing here all winter?'

"Captain Olson came back early from Florida the spring of 1964, but told me he'd had enough and was going to retire. He had never married and had always saved his money, so he didn't need to keep sailing. Partly on his recommendation, I started the season as relief captain and sailed as first mate on the *E.J. Block*, where Captain David Kinnear had instructions to let me take over. He was the fellow whose monkey Captain Walsh threw off the boat when I was second mate on the *L.E. Block,* so we knew one another pretty well, but he didn't like it that there were two or three other mates with more time in ratings that he thought should make captain before I did, so he gave me a lot of static about it.

"Finally, I asked to speak with him in his office. I said I was there with orders to take over and that was what I intended to do. If he had a problem with that, I told him I'd go to the fleet office. After that, he sat back in his chair and never said another word about my lack of seniority. I became one of the first of the fleet's young-blood captains that season. The *E.J. Block* was a good ship to learn on because it had no bowthruster and required careful handling in the Indiana Harbor ship canal and through the five bridges area that connected the harbor to Lake Michigan."

Once Paquette had proven himself capable of handling the ship, the fleet transferred Captain Kinnear to the *Philip D. Block* and Captain Paquette became master of the *E.J. Block*, where he immediately began implementing changes based on the experience he'd gained from serving with all of the masters who'd gone before him.

CHAPTER FOUR

Be My Guest

Given his fascination with weather, it's not surprising that one of the first things that 36-year-old Captain Dudley Paquette did upon assuming command in 1964 as permanent captain on the *E.J. Block* was to insist on routine monitoring and charting of weather reports and insisting that his mates practice regularly at using the radar, so that they would trust it and know what they were seeing when the scope was needed for navigating in foul weather. In fact, his one-time vessel agent and longtime friend Jerry Lawson laughingly remembers that Paquette's mates often seemed to have a permanent ring around their eyes from keeping their heads fastened to the viewing scope of the radar.

But first, the new captain of the *E.J. Block* found that he needed to saunter aft for a jawing of the cook, whom he describes as a tough old curmudgeon from Kewaunee, Wisconsin.

"Through the years, I always seemed to have to remind cooks who was captain. I also found it useful to indicate to them that I was tougher than they wanted to find out. With this character, I told him that I had an accounting background and would be watching his grocery bills and I didn't want to catch him playing the ponies or doing anything else on those bills. I also told him not to let me catch him giving the ship's food to his buddies on the dock, because he had so many friends that sometimes it seemed like more food was going over the side than we used for the crew. Finally, I said I wanted him to keep food available at all times for crewmen on watches, which had not been his practice before that.

He didn't like it much, but I was captain and signed his bills, so what could he do?

"Through all the years I put in as an officer, I've dealt with all kinds of people, but the cooks were a breed to themselves – tough and sometimes mean, especially the ones whose wives served with them in the galley. But, I figured out pretty early that if something was too tough or nobody else wanted it, it was just right for me."

And, as he had observed when first assigned as a third mate, the comfort, entertainment and well-being of guests now became an important part of his responsibility as captain.

On his first voyage as permanent captain of the *E.J. Block*, Paquette notes that a group of guests included a lady who was into ceramics. He still treasures a large ceramic replica of a lighthouse with a working light that she fashioned as a memento of their trip together and it has a place of honor in his home.

"I met many wonderful people that ranged from our own company officers to the CEO of AT&T and a number of politicians. I always felt privileged to serve as their host on ships where I served and I like to think that I helped sell a helluva lot of Inland products by giving those guests a great impression of the company. But they could create problems for you that had to be handled with kid gloves."

He also remembers that the best of intentions and advice didn't always yield perfect results. One time, he came on deck and spotted a lady guest sunning. "I warned her to be careful because the sun would be more intense than she was used to ashore," he says. "I got busy with other things and sort of forgot about her, but later in the afternoon, she was so sunburned they had to almost peel her nylon stockings loose from her legs and she had a couple of painful days before the sunburn healed enough to just be uncomfortable.

"As company officials, some of the guests had absolute power over our careers and many of the others were important customers of the company, so you wanted every one of them to have a perfect trip with you – but, man, you could get in some situations where you had to be a Philadelphia lawyer to keep from getting into trouble. I had a buzzer installed under the top of the dining room table and when things got too uncomfortable, I'd buzz four times, which meant that the bridge was to call me and request my presence in the pilothouse," he says.

"You could never relax as captain and guests added to the stress by creating all kinds of social pressure," he says, then notes that an episode years later when he was captain of the fleet flagship

On his first voyage as a captain, Paquette was host to a party of guests on the E.J. Block that included a woman who did ceramics. She devised this model of a working lighthouse for Captain Paquette, which is still a cherished memento of their trip together.

required particular diplomacy with a major Inland Steel executive and convinced Captain Paquette to take retirement as early as possible.

"This guy could just wink and your career would be over, so I was shocked one evening when he'd had way too much wine before dinner and said to me, 'Captain, I've always had the feeling that I am competing with you for the love of my wife.'

"It just shocked me. What in hell was I going to say to handle this? This was two or three years before I was eligible for my pension and, if I didn't handle it absolutely properly, I probably wouldn't make it. I'd never done anything with his wife that I wouldn't do for any guest, of course, and he was obviously pretty tipsy, but everyone at the table had heard it and I was just thunderstruck. His wife was embarrassed and I kind of turned it into a joke, but I quickly buzzed four times and made my escape a minute or two later. It bothered the hell out of me and, even after he sort of half apologized the next day, I was very uncomfortable. I told myself then and there that I'd take my pension just as soon as I was eligible, because you never knew when something might pop up and you couldn't joke or talk your way out of it."

But through his career as captain, Paquette says guests provided him with some of his best and the funniest of memories.

"The women, especially, made life interesting," he smiles. "As captain, I was always at the head of the table for dinner each night and I'd seat a lady on each side of me. The ladies saw it as an honor and most of the time they made life at sea a lot more fun than it would otherwise have been."

He says that the stewards who were assigned to the guest quarters could make the captain look especially capable with his guests.

"One of the best guest stewards I ever met was a guy named Jose Rodrigues from Brownsville, Texas," Paquette says. "He was really accommodating to me and the guests and every morning at

Following his first season as captain on the E.J. Block, *Captain Paquette was reassigned as captain of the old* Joseph Block, *which he describes as a "good boat," even though it was nearly 60 years old.*

0545, he'd have lightly toasted homemade bread and hot coffee waiting for me on the bridge. I'd go up in my robe and pajamas to that great view from the pilothouse windows and have my toast and coffee while I caught up with what had happened overnight.

"Jose was so good that I swear the guests would tip him $800 or a $1,000 a trip and I finally felt that I had to tell the guests to use a little discretion when tipping – they were our guests, after all, and he was getting paid wages for everything he did for them. Anyway, Jose ended up putting his wife through college and then setting up a bridal shop for her to run in Brownsville. I never really heard what became of him, but he always made sure our guests had the best time possible on our boat."

Getting back to his first season as a captain of the *E.J. Block*, Paquette especially remembers the last two trips of the 1964 season because both were to his hometown, Marquette. The first trip found them in a stiff northwest gale as they came upbound from the Soo in December.

"We were in a 35 to 45 mph wind that was pushing water over our bow and you talk about rolling and snow blowing up a squall – but I knew Marquette Harbor like my own hand and there's a nice sand beach I knew I could run her onto if need be, so I was flying when we came around the end of the breakwall out of that storm. I

Not every trip proved to be routine and the occasional opportunity to render assistance could lift morale for crewmen beginning to weary of their workaday schedules.

dropped both my bow and stern anchors to slow us down as we made for the dock and we got her tied up. We were there for four or five days taking on a load of frozen ore from Ishpeming they called Greenwood lump and the Marquette newspaper caught wind that I was captain and did a story about 'Local Boy Makes Good.' Several of my old boyhood friends came down to be sure it was really me. I guess they just couldn't believe that I'd ever amount to much of anything, after all the pranks we pulled as kids. Of course, almost all of them had sailed at one time or another, so they understood what was involved in making captain.

"On our way down from Marquette, we were surprised to see the old *Joe Block* as we rounded Whitefish Point. She was heading to Marquette for ore, but had anchored in Whitefish Bay out of the weather. After we got unloaded at Indiana Harbor, I was surprised to get orders to go back up to Marquette and pick up the cargo that Old *Joe* was sent up there for, because the captain of Old *Joe* didn't like the weather.

"After finishing that trip without incident and making a success of that first season, the fleet office told me that the captain of the *Joe Block,* who had more seniority than I did, complained bitterly that I was a new captain and had a newer, better boat than he did. I told the office I didn't give a damn what boat they gave me and to let him have the *E.J. Block*, if he wanted her. The next year, I was assigned as master of the *Joseph Block* and that was just fine with me

63

JOSEPH L. BLOCK
30 WEST MONROE STREET
CHICAGO 60603

September 4, 1973

Captain Dudley J. Paquette
STR. EDWARD L. RYERSON
Inland Steel Company
East Chicago, Indiana

Dear Captain Paquette:

Attached hereto are the pictures for the guest book on the RYERSON to be used on the two pages that we reserved, as well as a sketch showing a suggested arrangement. Thank you for taking care of this matter.

As you know, all members of my party and I thoroughly enjoyed our trip on the RYERSON and, again, thank you and all members of the crew for the many kind attentions bestowed on us.

With every good wish, in which Mrs. Block joins,

Sincerely,

Joseph L. Block

because I knew the ship was seaworthy and had modern equipment. I was master on her for three good seasons before she was wrecked and it was especially nice when Mr. Joseph Block, himself, would sail with us on the boat. Old *Joe* was always a good ship for me but, then, I always kept a good attitude about everything and figured when somebody didn't like what I did, I'd be damned sure to make them wish they'd kept out of my way."

September 3, 1975

Dear Dudley:

Following our pleasant trip with you in July,
I had copies made of a few of my Polaroad pictures.

I'm enclosing one of the two of us as it
seemed a good likeness of yourself.

Yours,

Fred

Captain Dudley Paquette
SS WILFRED SYKES
Plant No. 2 Dock Office
INDIANA HARBOR 2-700

*Showing he was host to some of the most powerful businessmen in the
country, Captain Paquette has scrapbooks of letters like these from Inland
Steel officials Joseph L. Block and Frederick Jaicks.*

After the old *Joseph Block* was damaged on a shoal while he was
on funeral leave early in the 1968 season, the fleet made Paquette
its relief captain to replace masters who were on vacation.

"That was a great experience because I was captain on a
number of ships with different handling and equipment," he says.
"In fact, the only Inland ships I didn't relieve on were my two
favorites, the *Sykes* and the *Ryerson.*"

65

The 1969 season saw him again assigned as master of the *E.J. Block*, but he also served temporarily as relief captain on the *L.E. Block*, where he was permanently assigned for the 1970 season, when a steel strike was threatened but proved to be a fairly routine season.

The following year (1971) the company decided to put new cargo holds into the *L.E. Block* and Paquette spent considerable time during that year at the shipyard in Manitowoc, Wisconsin, where he chafed at being stuck ashore at the shipyard – despite accommodations in the bridal suite at the Manitowoc Hotel. Thus, he was glad that fall when the company requested that he meet the *Wilfred Sykes* at Indiana Harbor and relieve the captain on that ship.

Paquette chuckles and says, "The old captain, who was nicknamed 'The Chicken of the Sea,' was anchored in bad weather in the Straits of Mackinaw, saying he didn't want any more storms in his life. I took over as relief captain on November 24 and, ironically, our first trip to Thunder Bay and back was under the influence of a high pressure system the whole trip and we hardly saw a ripple. The Chicken of the Sea was kind of embarrassed that he'd gotten off before that trip.

"The next year, I was glad to be permanently assigned as master of the *Sykes*, which was still one of Inland's show boats, and over the next two years we took out a fantastic group of guests. Of course, we got the flag upside down one time and it would be Inland Steel's grand old man, Mr. Joseph Block, that spotted it and told us about it."

With a long list of Inland's most important company officials and major customers as guests on the *Sykes* during the next several seasons, Paquette especially remembers that Frederick Jaicks, the chairman of Inland Steel, always told people that boarded as his guests, "This is the only place in the company where I'm not the boss," meaning that the captain remained all-powerful aboard his ship – even with the man who with a wave of his hand could otherwise have had him demoted or removed from service.

But it wasn't always the power of the guest that made long-lasting memories. "One of the more memorable trips I made was with a party of eight ladies as guests," he remembers. "It was a little unusual to have guest parties with women only, but I did have one now and then. Anyway, this party dressed to the teeth every night for the captain's dinner and every one of them wanted to sit next to me at the table, so I put eight numbers in my hat and had them draw each evening for the seats next to me. They all liked to have a good time and were fun, so they really made that trip memorable for all of us."

While every guest carries special memories of their days aboard a Great Lakes ore carrier, likely the one guest with the strongest impression was the wife of the relief chief engineer who was temporarily assigned to the *Sykes* on the trip of November 9-11, 1975.

Paquette laughs as he tells the story, "It was more than a month after the time of year when we'd take out VIP guests, but crewmen were allowed to bring their families for a trip and he was a replacement, so he probably didn't have a chance to have his wife with him earlier in the season.

"Her husband's quarters were aft in the boat and we didn't see much of her, except for meals. Once the storm started, I didn't really have time to worry about her – there wouldn't have been much I could have done, even if I had thought of it.

"After we left the *Fitz* search area, the Chief told us his wife got worried when she started seeing water washing over the porthole in his quarters in the early part of the trip out of Thunder Bay. He said that she crawled into the bunk and was laying spread-eagled when the storm really started howling and the porthole was being washed almost constantly. The real topper, though, was when we hit the trough of the seas as we turned around during the search. She told him that the porthole was completely under water and she just flipped out.

"When we got into Indiana Harbor at the end of the trip, she made him leave the boat and I heard that he never went back aboard another ore freighter."

CHAPTER FIVE

Building Seas

On December 15, 1974, Captain Paquette laid up the *Sykes* at Fraser Shipyards in Superior, Wisconsin, where the ship was scheduled to be converted from a straight decker to a self-unloader. He remembers it as one instance where good ship handling produced a laugh. "Bobby Fraser had spent $25,000 or $30,000 to modify a dock at the shipyard that they thought would be in the way when I was getting the *Sykes* into the work place, but I brought her in, moved her into place and was nowhere near the area where they'd torn the dock out. As we were tying up, I looked down from the deck and had to laugh, because Bobby was standing there with his hands on his head, thinking of all the money he'd spent needlessly."

"The company sent me and my chief engineer to Canada to examine a self-unloading system that used an endless belt. They didn't spare any expense on that conversion," he says. "In addition to cargo hold modifications and installation of the unloading boom and conveyor belt system, we also had a 1,000-horsepower Caterpillar diesel bow thruster installed, so the boat was much more maneuverable and self-sufficient in tight situations."

The length of shipping seasons had been expanding and, after laying up the *Sykes*, his 1974 season stretched into January 1975 when he reported aboard the *Ryerson* early that month and finally laid it up on January 25.

In many ways, the year 1975 was a watershed in the American steel industry. Tonnages of cargo remained above 90 million tons a season in the early half of the decade and many smaller and specialty steel companies like Youngstown Sheet and Tube, Interlake Iron and Jones and Laughlin created a brisk demand for ore above and beyond that of bigger, better known producers like U.S. Steel, Bethlehem, Inland, Republic and Armco. Before the smaller and specialty producers were merged, bought out or went bankrupt in the later 1970s and early 1980s, they were important customers of both the transportation and the iron ore industries.

Optimism about the future of steel rode high in the eastern offices of steel executives. A measure of that optimism is the fact that steel companies invested billions of dollars in new 1,000-foot ore boats and additional iron ore production facilities to fill the holds of those ships. Shipyards on the Great Lakes had a waiting list for new ships and an absolute boom hit northeastern Minnesota, as a crush of construction workers from throughout America flooded in for the outstanding wages being paid at the numerous projects to renovate, expand and build new taconite processing facilities. Over about a four-year period in the mid- to late 1970s, something in the range of 20-30 million tons of production capacity was added at properties on the Mesabi Iron Range. Steel companies believed they would shortly require that added ore to meet future demands.

And, even though a new generation of ships and a new era in shipping had been introduced with the 1972 launch of Bethlehem Steel's 1,000-foot motor vessel (M/V) *Stewart J. Cort,* followed a few weeks later by U.S. Steel's 858-foot M/V *Roger Blough,* and the 1973 introduction of the 1,000-foot tug-barge *Presque Isle,* many of the smaller boats that would be scrapped or indefinitely laid up within a few years were still sailing majestically on their rounds, occasionally hauling coal upbound to Lake Superior ports, but always deeply laden with iron ore on their downbound leg and always operating on the principal of delivering cargo as quickly and cheaply as possible. As the 1,000-footers became more numerous, each replacing from three to five of the smaller ships and putting as many as 120 seamen out of work, the sailor's career became less predictable. Where once there had been jobs for anyone willing to sail, now the companies had backlogs of unemployed sailors.

But all of that was of secondary interest to Captain Dudley Paquette, whose focus in 1975 fixes on June 29, when the conversion of the *Sykes* was complete and he took command at Superior for her trials as the fleet's first self-unloader.

"We had a lot of shipyard people with us and had some breakdowns and the usual problems, but the ship passed the tests and I took her into service in early July. Even though she was 25 or 26 years old, I really thought of her as a brand new ship, because we could do so many things we couldn't do before the conversion. I also noticed that the conversion work seemed to have stiffened her quite a bit and she had a good solid feel to her – but then I always wanted to feel good about the boats I mastered."

After a couple of months of getting familiar with the nuances of the newly converted *Sykes*, he relieved the captain of the *Ryerson* for six weeks, then reported back to the *Sykes* on October 21 and stayed aboard through the end of the season – thus being uniquely positioned for the drama during the saga of the *Edmund Fitzgerald*.

* * *

And that drama was far from over when northwest winds knocked down the wild northeast seas as Paquette departed from the vicinity of Passage Island at 3:45 p.m. on November 10. Taking the lead as the *Sykes* and *Blough* began the southeastern journey from the northern end of Isle Royale, Paquette remembers that the seas built steadily from the northwest through the gathering darkness of late afternoon, creating a following sea with more prominent swells and waves as the storm continued its counterclockwise rotation.

The "skip" of radio signals was such that the bridge was able to hear occasional bits of radio communication from the *Fitzgerald* and the *Anderson*, both of which had changed course in the late morning to follow the eastern shoreline downbound for Whitefish Bay west of the Soo. Although they did find moderating winds as they began the southerly leg of their journey, experienced sailors know that this was merely the eye of the storm system, an odd, calm center that sailors call the "sucker hole." As the storm continued traveling to the northeast, the backside of the system produced mounting winds that swung around to hit them from the northwest. The two ships now found themselves sailing with increasing seas building on their starboard quarter, crashing diagonally with mounting fury against the right or starboard side of the aft area of the hull.

"As I said earlier, boats function best in heavy seas that come directly at the bow and the second best is following seas that come directly at the stern. With a following sea that pushed us along pretty briskly, we were now committed to proceed downbound, but, as the winds and seas built, I'm sure that some of the crew were telling themselves that only a damned fool would be out there. My decision to leave the safety of Thunder Bay wasn't mentioned by

Oglebay Norton Company

Self-unloading ore carriers utilize a system of gates in the cargo hold to feed iron pellets onto continuous belts that convey the ore onto the boom, which is swung over the side to deliver the load to the dock.

anybody in the pilothouse, of course – that just wouldn't be proper on a ship's bridge. I was the captain and it was my job to make decisions like this, based on the best information and my own experience. I was confident that I had a good picture of what to expect and we had already seen the wind come around to our stern, so my decision to proceed downbound was based on solid thinking, but the length that this low pressure system would influence the storm was somewhat longer than I had calculated."

In his testimony before the Marine Board, the *Anderson's* Captain Cooper stated that he encountered seas of 25 to 35 feet about 10 to 15 miles southeast of the lee of Caribou Island. Sailing in the open sea, well to the west of Cooper's route, Paquette says the *Sykes* encountered similar seas, but that his southeastern heading had the ship at the most advantageous angle it could have sailed to handle those seas.

As the seas built the first couple of hours of their journey, they turned off 'Iron Mike,' the automatic pilot, and were steering manually to maintain a better feel for the effect that the mounting seas were having on the ship. His bridge watch kept busy observing the effects of the wind and waves as the *Sykes* made way through the early evening hours.

"About 1700 hours (5 p.m.), the mate said, 'The seas are clearing our stern, Cap,' and I glanced back to see green water – the powerful center of a wave – not only overtake us, but wash completely over our after boat deck, which is the highest point at the stern of a ship and 20 to 25 feet above the waterline. Since we

71

were making normal speed and were easily being overtaken by the waves, these huge seas were going to stay with us for a while."

Plowing ahead on the open lake with huge waves washing forward over the weather deck, he knew he was sailing in conditions that would become legend, but had no way of knowing how legendary.

Paquette says, "At 1800 hours, the growing northwest seas were serious enough that I made a radio call to Neal Rolfson, who confirmed winds registering 60 knots from 290 degrees – precisely the northwester I had expected.

"All we could do was continue on our course and watch green water climb over our stern and splash over the hatches on its way toward us," Paquette says. "I had given orders that no one was to be out on deck, of course, and was satisfied that our inspection prior to leaving Thunder Bay had been thorough, but I told the watchmen to keep a sharp eye out for anything unusual because it never hurts to keep everybody alert."

Darkness had fallen some hours before and now snow swirled out of the night in blinding squalls that obliterated sight of the after lights – even those illuminating the stack and its colors – as well as the safety lights illuminating the access ladderway from the pilothouse to the upper deck.

The soft glow of the radars added to the eerie feeling of isolation on the bridge as the mate logged, "Seas continue to overtake us and come aboard from each side. The seas climb over the stern and slam back together amidships, flowing forward before they spill back into the lake."

Almost as an afterthought, the mate also noted a break in heavy snow and somewhat later logged observation of the huge seas piling up on the port (left) lifeboat – located on the boat or upper deck at the stern.

"Later," Paquette says, "after the storm eased and we were able to get out on deck, we discovered that the strongback, a 2-by-4-inch wooden framework that supports the canvas cover on the lifeboat, was broken by either that wave or one following it that washed completely over the whole damned stern."

About the same time that he estimates the strongback being broken by boarding waves, the engine room rang up the pilothouse and reported that the Draft-O-Meters (instruments that the first mate uses to trim or level the boat during loading) had been broken at both ends of the weather deck by the massive seas.

"It didn't affect us at this point and was nothing catastrophic," Captain Paquette says. "I had full confidence in our watertight fastenings and we were riding well in deep water but, being a navigator, I double-checked our position and noted on radar that we were about 35 miles east-northeast of Keweenaw Point – right in the middle of the whole damned lake."

He pauses, puffs his cheeks and continues, "Silence is the usual response to heavy weather by the bridge watch. They pride themselves on being completely professional, and I'll say that I had never really seen or felt fear in a pilothouse before that night. It wouldn't have been noticeable to an outsider, but it was there during this trip. As captain, I did not dare show concern, of course, but I'll admit I'd never seen or been in anything like this in all my years of sailing – even on that old slow freighter (the *Newell*) in the Atlantic during World War II."

Looking back, he says, "From the bits of the conversation we could pick up on the radios that afternoon and evening, we knew that the *Anderson* and *Fitz* were taking a beating from those quartering seas as they proceeded southward. The first clue we had that it was much more serious came at about 2145 (9:45 p.m.) when we were shocked to hear the Coast Guard come in loud and clear with the report that the SS *Edmund Fitzgerald* was reported missing and requesting all ships in the area to join a search and rescue effort."

Captain Paquette pauses, looks back in time and says, "I didn't mention it to anyone and it sure the hell didn't make me feel good, but I couldn't help remembering that I'd told Lee Ward the night before on our trip up to Thunder Bay that they were going to get into trouble."

He says that there really wasn't much solid information about the *Fitzgerald* through most of the next two seasons. What little there was came from newspapers and radio, but the rumors kept flying.

"I came to the conclusion that the ship developed a stress fracture in the storm as a result of Captain McSorley pushing it in those massive quartering seas, but nobody involved in the investigation seemed to think that was the case."

And despite the severity of this storm, he notes, Captain Ernest McSorley's ship handling in this situation was likely the same as always, since the master of the *Fitzgerald* was known for pushing the big, powerful ship as fast as possible in any seas – even when other ships took cover. That assessment was buttressed by the late Glen Burke, a veteran employee at the former Reserve Mining Company in Silver Bay, Minnesota, who has always harbored a special interest in the wreck of the *Fitzgerald,* which loaded at Reserve hundreds of times on a regular basis through the years.

"I shot the breeze with the crewmen, I ate on the boat a couple of times when mates invited me and I helped tie it up when it would come in during bad weather," Burke said. "I saw it come and go during storms when no other boats were sailing. His own mates told me that McSorley was money-hungry and would sail no matter what the weather was like."

Such exploits, admits Captain Paquette, made McSorley a shipowner's ideal. In McSorley's 25th season with a master's rating and the youngest person to hold that license when he received it in 1950 at 38 years of age, he had served 44 years as a mariner, starting on salt water as an 18-year-old deckhand. His record was basically unblemished.

"Every captain knew it was his job to deliver cargo as cheaply and as quickly as possible and, if you didn't measure up, the company would replace you with a captain who would measure up," Paquette says. "But you were also responsible for the safety and security of your ship and your crew, and I always believed that that responsibility took precedence over any other concern."

Robert Hom, an executive with the Duluth (Minnesota) Entertainment Convention Center, was a deckhand, deck watch and occasional wheelman on the SS *Armco* during the 1970 and part of the 1971 sailing seasons while McSorley was captain and also got acquainted with a number of sailors who went on to be crewmen on the *Fitzgerald* when it was lost. Hom's description of the captain is considerably kinder than Burke's and Paquette's, noting that McSorley was easy to work for and went out of his way to help sailors who showed an interest in navigation.

"He was a quiet guy out on deck. He'd just answer your questions, but wasn't a guy who got into long conversations," Hom says. "In the pilothouse, with just the guys on watch, he had a great sense of humor and was very easy to get along with."

Hom says that the *Armco* did go to shelter occasionally while he served on the boat, but that McSorley also pushed through some serious seas. "I believe there was a tonnage bonus for captains in those days and it paid for captains to sail in heavy weather, shorten their trips, load as heavy as possible and try to get in an extra trip or two during a season."

"I never had the feeling that he was reckless, but he did like to keep the fleet office happy," Hom analyzes.

Asked if McSorley ever expressed any interest in being master of the *Fitzgerald*, he says, "I know that while I was on the *Armco*, I thought it was odd that he never once went to visit on the

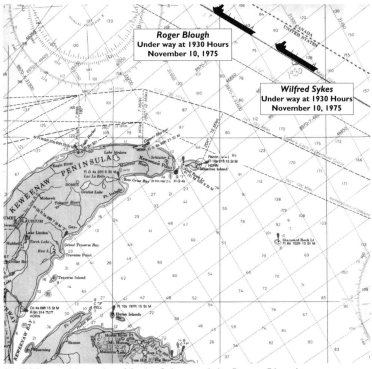

By 7:30 p.m. November 10, the Sykes and the Roger Blough were northeast of the tip of the Keweenaw Peninsula, with monstrous seas breaking over their sterns and howling winds pushing them on the way.

Fitzgerald, even though we were in the same port to load or unload a number of times. I don't think the *Fitz* would have been a prize to him. For one thing, with guests aboard, he'd have to wear his captain's uniform and that just wasn't his style."

The assignment of this seasoned, company-oriented captain to the big, powerful, speedy *Edmund Fitzgerald* would seem to be a perfect match. The ship was 14 years old when he took over – virtually new by Great Lakes standards – and would carry huge tonnages of cargo as it outran every other ore carrier of its time. The master had a wide variety of experience and had proven he would do whatever he could to achieve the profitable status the company demanded of its vessels and captains.

But Captain Paquette says this captain and this machine may have formed an ill-fated combination that led to events that claimed the ship and its crew.

"When I talked a minute ago about old-time captains, I was talking about guys who first mastered ships that were much less powerful than the *Fitz*," he says. "A major problem was that those senior masters came off boats with maybe 1,500 or 2,000 horsepower and took over boats like the *Fitzgerald*, with 7,000 or more horsepower, but they never received enough training in ship handling to properly use that much power.

"It's like taking somebody with a perfect record driving Ford Escorts and putting them in a race car. That driver might be able to operate the car in first gear on a flat roadway in nice weather, but is pretty sure to get in trouble if he increases his speed and gets involved in hills, rain or snow, curves and other hazards.

"Ship handling is about common sense and your feel for a boat. Common sense comes into play when you plot a course that keeps you as sheltered as possible. Then, if your touch or feel for the boat tells you the ship is straining and laboring, you check down your speed to relieve the stress on the boat.

"In the case of the *Fitzgerald*, I believe McSorley kept pushing the boat full speed ahead much longer than was prudent in the heavy seas he was taking and he sure as hell used poor judgment in the course he set early in that trip. In my opinion, all of the subsequent events arose because he kept pushing that ship and didn't have enough training in weather forecasting to use common sense and pick a route out of the worst of the wind and seas.

"But then, he had pushed the *Fitz* through bad weather so many times that I think he just figured the boat would take it and get him through."

But there were apparently aspects of the ship's performance that McSorley did find disturbing. In his book, *Lake Superior Shipwrecks*, Dr. Julius F. Wolff Jr. first notes that McSorley was "known as a 'weather captain' more than willing to be out when others were in, (although) there is little doubt of his skills as a vessel master." Wolff then continues by quoting Marine Board testimony from former *Fitzgerald* Second Mate Richard Orgel, who served aboard the ship in 1972-73. Orgel told the board that the ship had an unusual action that McSorley called "the wiggling thing." According to his statement, this action consisted of bending, whipping, twisting and springing "like a diving board after somebody has jumped off."

In particular, Orgel remembered a storm in November 1973 when he was especially surprised by the ship's reaction to seas of about 10 feet. "By looking aft, there was quite a bit of action there. She bends and springs considerably."

And, although this was not a particularly memorable storm by Lake Superior standards, when McSorley left the bridge he is reported to have said to the mate, "If she starts to do the wiggling thing, let me know. This thing scares me sometimes."

Orgel said the phenomenon did occur later and McSorley ordered him to change course and check down the speed.[4]

A copyright story by Larry Oakes in the November 10, 1997, edition of the *Star-Tribune* newspaper of Minneapolis, Minnesota, also quotes Orgel as saying that he once complimented the *Fitzgerald* to the captain and said that it must be a comfort to have a big, beautiful, fast ship, after mastering older, slower boats like his first command in 1951 on the SS *Carrollton*.

"McSorley said to me, 'Not as great as you might think. The *Carrollton* would beat you up some, but she could take it and bring you in,'" Orgel said, noting that the captain implied that he did not entirely trust the *Fitzgerald*.[5]

Captain Paquette addresses the last statement first, saying, "His old ship might have made 11 or 12 miles an hour and had maybe 2,000 horsepower – probably not enough so he could push the boat very hard in a serious storm – but here he was, making maybe 16 or 17 miles an hour with three or four times the horsepower to push it through that storm. That was putting a tremendous strain on that ship's structure.

"November 9 and 10, 1975, was just typical for him. I was right across the dock from him and he was loaded right to the line, was out the entry and full speed ahead while his deck crew was still replacing hatch covers and he chose to sail the shortest route, despite the weather information and advisories he was receiving – and he continued pretty much at full speed ahead through those huge seas until about 1530 (3:30 p.m.) on November 10, when he reported to Captain Cooper that his ship had deck damage and a starboard list and he was checking down his speed so that the *Anderson* could close up with him.

"I doubt he'd have been able to do that on his former boats. They just wouldn't have had the power to pound ahead in such seas."

Paquette turns his attention to Orgel's other comments about McSorley and the *Fitzgerald*. While McSorley's competence was never questioned by the Marine Board and NTSB, which found no fault on anyone's part for the foundering, and virtually every other reference to his 25-year career as a captain has been couched in complimentary terms, Orgel's testimony adds credibility to Captain Paquette's assertion that McSorley may have contributed to the tragedy by ignoring some of the primary responsibilities of a good ship master.

"First and foremost, the captain's primary duty is to ensure that his ship is safe and seaworthy – no matter how much pressure he feels the company putting on him to keep to his schedule and keep his budget in line. If McSorley had any misgivings about the way his ship handled or reacted to heavy weather, he was the one with the responsibility to check it out and get it fixed, but there is no indication he made any effort to do that. Nobody, from the CEO of the company to the office boy, wants to have a tragedy like the *Fitzgerald* on their hands and it's the master's job to keep it from happening."

Asked his thoughts about the "wiggling thing" that Orgel described, Captain Paquette says, "The first thing I'd think of would be a keel problem – since the keel is the backbone of a boat and holds everything in place. Some ships do have peculiarities – remember what I said about needing a really tender touch with the *Philip Block* because she was so limber and springy after being lengthened – but with a relatively new ship like the *Fitz*, which had not really been modified from its original design, you wouldn't expect that sort of thing, unless something was wrong – and I'd think first about the keel.

"If I were captain of a ship that acted funny and I couldn't figure out why, I'd request an inspection to see what was going on – and if any boat had ever scared me, I'd have laid it up until somebody found out what was wrong and fixed it.

"From everything I knew and heard about him, if McSorley was so worried about the action of the *Fitz* that he ordered a mate to check down their speed and change course in 10-foot seas, that proves to me beyond a doubt that he was afraid of his own boat, because it just wasn't in his nature as a captain to slow down or change from the shortest route to his destination.

"I've also wondered if it might be possible that he just wasn't suited to captain a boat any longer, because the cook/ship watcher (Burgner in his 1977 deposition) said that McSorley was concerned about his wife's health and was mainly interested in getting to retirement. It's very possible that he came up on empty that last season and was just toughing it out to get the best pension he could. "

Stated as succinctly as possible, Burgner said in his deposition that Captain McSorley "beat hell" out of the boat and seldom "hauled down" (slowed or stopped) for weather, unlike the previous master, Captain Peter Pulcer, who would look for the safest,

As a new ship, the Fitzgerald *drew attention wherever it went and graciously hosted many guests through the years it was in service. Big, fast and powerful, it delivered millions of tons of iron ore before it sank.*

smoothest route to sail and often anchored in storm conditions, which he said McSorley rarely did. Burgner also testified that McSorley seemed unable or unwilling to confront mates and insist that they keep up with routine maintenance. In contrast, Burgner testified, Pulcer harassed the mates and men until necessary maintenance work was completed. Burgner said that McSorley's apparent inattention led to low morale among crew members on the *Fitzgerald* that last season, as the captain's lack of interest rubbed off on the crew – all of which seems to support Captain Paquette's questioning of his fitness to serve as a captain.[6]

To illustrate his contention, Burgner related what looms as a key conversation he claimed to have heard during the summer of 1975 between McSorley and crew members who had been "de-mudding" ballast tanks in the keel level at the very bottom of the *Fitzgerald*. Burgner said the crewmen came up on deck and told the captain that the keel was loose again and McSorley said, "All this SOB has to do is stay together one more year. After that, I don't (care) what happens to it."

Finally, in other observations of affairs aboard the ship, Burgner seemed to verify Orgel's description of a peculiar action, saying that the bow would hook to one side or the other in heavy seas and not return in the time it normally takes a ship to recover. "[On] the *Fitzgerald*, it seemed like the bow would just never get back there again and another (wave) would hit it: she'd go back over again.... She had an awful lot of movement to her."

He also testified that the ship groaned more than most ships – indeed, it made a sound he'd never heard on any other ship in his long experience at sea.

Burgner's deposition also lends support to Captain Paquette's assertion that the *Fitzgerald* was unlikely to have shoaled near Caribou Island, one of the wreck theories. His testimony describes McSorley as a navigator who was knowledgeable and experienced on Lake Superior. In addition, the record shows that the captain and all three mates held pilots' licenses for the Great Lakes and First Mate John H. McCarthy held a masters' license for 34 years and had his own command for a period of time. That means that at least two experienced, licensed navigators were on the bridge at the time that the *Fitzgerald* passed the shoals and Caribou Island.

Owing his life to the fact that he got off the *Edmund Fitzgerald* with foot trouble in the late summer before the sinking, Burgner had sailed more than 30 seasons for Oglebay Norton and served 10 years as chief steward (cook) on the *Fitzgerald*, also spending each winter from 1966 through 1973 as ship watcher after the ship was laid up in his hometown of Superior, Wisconsin. Despite that background, he was not called or made available for either the Marine Board or the NTSB investigations, instead giving his deposition in December 1977 to the law firm representing the families of Alan Kalmon and Blaine Wilhelm, both of whom perished in the wreck.

In the deposition, he relates that he told Oglebay Norton officials and attorneys after the wreck that he knew the ship had a "loose keel" and they told him to say nothing to anyone about the ship or accident, to contact them if anyone wanted to talk to him about it, make no contact with the Marine Board or Coast Guard and to simply stay in Texas, where he had gone after retiring from the company.

Given his gritty, often acrimonious history with ships' cooks, it seems ironic that Captain Paquette finds the information from George Burgner's deposition credible.

He grins and says, "Oh sure, a cook might be tougher than hell

Eerily from more than 500 feet down, the underwater cameras aboard the first submerged explorations captured the name of the sunken freighter, providing proof that the wreckage was indeed the missing ship.

and mean – and they sure aren't paid to know anything about ship handling or design and construction – but they're a critical part of the crew. Everybody on the boat has to go to the galley three times a day to eat and the galley crew has plenty of chances to chew the fat with crewmen, so cooks are usually pretty well tuned into what's going on aboard a ship."

Despite his overall interest in Burgner's testimony, Captain Paquette has no interest in Burgner's answers to inquiries by the lawyers about loading the ship. The captain says, "I loaded right beside the *Fitz* in Superior and there wasn't anything about that dock that the first mate and the captain of the *Fitz* wouldn't have seen many times in their careers. I've never had any thought that the boat was loaded badly or incorrectly."

One aspect of that portion of the deposition does strike his funny bone, however. The 1973 increase in draft authorized by the Coast Guard and American Bureau of Shipping required that a Loading Manual be issued for each vessel. While Coast Guard records indicated there was such a manual for the *Fitzgerald*, Burgner told the lawyers that in his time aboard the ship, he knew of no formal loading manual being used by mates when the boat was being loaded.

Instead, he said, the mates asked the galley staff for the cardboard stiffeners that came in the cooks' white uniform shirts when they came from the laundry. According to Burgner, the stiffeners were used to keep track of the loading sequence (how much ore is loaded in which hatches and when) as the ship was being laden. Once the ship was loaded, Burgner said these no-cost records were stowed in a drawer in the first mate's quarters, but were thrown away at the end of the season when the mate cleaned out his quarters.

Captain Paquette chuckles and says, "I've never heard of using the galley shirt cardboard to keep track of loading, but they would have just been thrown away and were stiff enough so you wouldn't need a clipboard, so the first mate was saving the cost of a notebook and a clipboard. But the loading that day was absolutely routine and professional and had no part at all in the loss of the *Fitz*."

Burgner's testimony also supports Captain Paquette's hypothesis about the hatch clamps. Saying that McSorley regularly sailed without the hatch covers being securely clamped down, even in foul weather, Burgner said that this was particularly true when overtime pay would be required for the deckhands accomplishing that work. (Significantly, the ship loaded in Superior, Wisconsin, on a Sunday, when overtime pay for deck crewmen was required. By their regular Monday shift, the ship was already beleaguered by foul weather.) Finally, he said McSorley was so cost-conscious that the deck crew did not even clean up taconite pellets that were spilled around the hatches during loading and unloading, if that cleanup would require overtime pay. As a result, crewmen routinely used the side tunnels for trips fore or aft until the cleanup was completed, rather than risk a fall from slipping on the marble-like pellets scattered on the deck.[7]

Captain Paquette says, "His deck crew was still placing hatch covers as the ship went out the Superior Entry onto Lake Superior, so it wouldn't surprise me if they fastened a minimum number of clamps as each cover was placed. I've done that myself when the ship was empty and the weather was going to be nice. Twelve clamps – two on each corner and four in the middle – is what we dogged down in those situations and it wouldn't surprise me at all if they left a lot of the clamps unfastened – because they were pretty late in getting their hatches covered up and they were sailing in good weather. But he should have known by then that more severe weather was forecast and I think you'd have to call it negligence if he sailed into a storm front on Lake Superior with a minimum number of hatch clamps dogged down, just because he'd have had to pay more overtime to get the rest of those clamps fastened down."

While no one will ever be able to testify that the hatch covers were or were not securely clamped and seaworthy, the photographic record provided by the several exploratory deep diving expeditions shows many hatch clamps that appear to be in perfect condition. Only a few clamps were damaged, which the Marine Board concluded probably were the only ones fastened and thus ineffective hatch closure contributed to the wreck. Together with the deposed testimony of George Burgner that McSorley often sailed with many hatch clamps unfastened and Captain Paquette's own admission that he commonly sailed in nice weather with a minimum of a dozen clamps secured, there does seem to be some reasonable basis for doubt about that subject.

CHAPTER SIX

Worrisome Wiggling

From deckhand, AB and wheelman on fresh and salt water to officer and captain of ships that moved millions of tons of material over the years, Captain Dudley Paquette offers a 32-year wealth of nautical lore and experience as support for his theory about the loss of the *Fitzgerald*. That background leads him to believe that Captain McSorley's tendency to run full speed ahead in heavy weather caused structural stress that resulted in a fracture of hull plates in what he calls the hinge area of the *Edmund Fitzgerald*. He describes the hinge as being the area where the greatest amount of flexing occurs when a ship is in heavy weather. It is located two-thirds aft of the bow and a third forward of the stern.

Paquette believes that the crack first leaked water into the Number 7 ballast tank in the hinge area, then deepened to invade other internal areas and deluged the inside of the *Fitzgerald* with water that its pumps could not – or were never designed to – evacuate fast enough to maintain trim. Continuous pounding by massive seas caused the fracture to deepen and spread, finally reaching a critical stage that allowed the stern to separate completely from the hold and bow sections. Later information and events would also raise a suspicion that the *Fitzgerald* itself may have had design or construction flaws that contributed to its demise. Until now, his opinion about the wreck has never been included in any writings about the sinking of the ship.

The Marine Board of Investigation did briefly consider the possibility of a stress fracture, but a panel of marine experts reviewing more than 19 hours of videotape taken by the Controlled Underwater Recovery Vehicle-III (CURV-III) during the spring of 1976 for the Coast Guard investigation of the wreck concluded that there was no visual evidence of such a "brittle fracture" in any wreckage that the panel could examine on the videotapes. The board also said that there was no correlation between such structural failure and the loss of vents and fence rail reported by McSorley. The Coast Guard board settled instead on ineffective hatch closures as the "most likely" cause of the foundering. As noted in Chapter 1, the Lake Carriers' Association argued that the ship was more likely to have been damaged by striking the shoals north of Caribou Island. A third theory for the sinking has the listing *Fitzgerald* being overtaken and overwhelmed by the so-called "Three Sisters," which are described as a combination of two large waves striking close together, followed by a larger third wave that smashes a vessel as it struggles to recover from the force of the preceding pair.

None of those possibilities mean, however, that there is no evidence supporting Captain Paquette's proposal that structural failure in the area of the Number 7 ballast tank caused the wreck of the *Fitzgerald* and it's quite feasible that a stress fracture in the "hinge area," as he calls it, might not appear in the early photos that were examined by the panel of marine experts, since so much of the wreckage has been described by several investigators as being all but unrecognizable and the video photography was at times obscured by mud that was stirred up by the CURV-III. And, the approximate 260 feet from the stern to the Number 7 ballast tank coincides closely with the estimated 250- to 285-foot section of inverted stern reported by the various investigative diving operations.

Historically, the Marine Board's record of damage and repair work on the *Fitzgerald* included a serious grounding in 1969 that resulted in damage to the bottom and internal superstructure of some consequence in the aft area of the ship, a 1970 collision with the SS *Hochelaga* that did damage above the waterline in somewhat the same area of the ship and three instances of damage above the waterline from collisions with lock walls at Sault Ste. Marie, Michigan. In addition, cracking of welds between the outer shell plating and the keelson (an interior stiffening system in the keel area of a ship) was discovered in 1969 and again in 1973 and repair work was done to patch these cracked welds during winter lay up in each of those years.

Besides these officially reported incidents of required repairs to the hull, Frederick J. Shannon's privately financed Expedition '94 Ltd. dives to the wreck produced 42 hours of videotape. He reported in the December 1995 *Michigan Natural Resources Magazine* that seven deep indentations in the bottom of the stern, which are identified in the Coast Guard's Marine Board report as buckles caused by the impact when the bow struck the lake bottom, are actually damage caused by grounding in shallow ports or river bottom damage – suggesting there may have been other instances of groundings that dented but did not penetrate the hull and, thus, went unreported.[8] In the 1996 updated edition of his 1977 bestseller, *The Wreck of the* Edmund Fitzgerald, Frederick Stonehouse rates the quality of Shannon's photography as excellent. The cameras examined the bow, the massive wreckage of the cargo area and the overturned stern in detail and the resulting photos show no evidence on the bottom of the stern, the propeller or the rudder of the ship that would indicate the ship struck a shoal, one of the wreck theories.[9]

After detailed study of the photographic evidence he collected, Shannon said in the magazine article that his team analyzed the collected evidence and determined that the ship broke on the surface and that the stern sank before the remainder of the ship, based on the fact that an eight-foot section of vent pipe and its cover were discovered lying atop the inverted stern. These vents were located on the weather deck forward of the stern, suggesting that the stern had already settled on the bottom by the time the bow slammed into the bottom and the cargo hold disintegrated.

Shannon also says that his team found that the distance between the intact stern and bow sections of the wreckage is 255 feet, some 85 feet farther apart than the Marine Board reported. Of that discovery, Shannon said, "This placement does not support the theory that the ship plunged to the bottom in one piece, breaking apart when it struck bottom. If this were true, the two sections would be much closer. In addition, the angle, repose and mounding of clay and mud at the site indicate the stern rolled over on the surface, spilling taconite ore pellets from its severed cargo hold, and then landed on portions of the cargo itself."

Regarding the official record of damage, Captain Paquette says, "Judging from my own experience, five incidents that involved hull damage in a five-year period pretty well tells the story of a ship that was getting banged around pretty hard. In 16 years as a captain, I only put a dent in one boat, when a 1,000-footer gave me a helluva

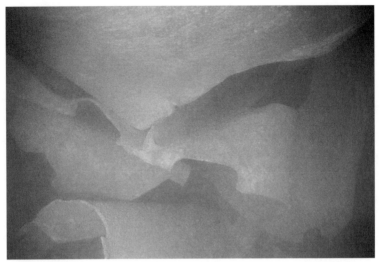

Twisted into grotesque patterns, the steel plates of the wreck provide a visual record of the tremendous forces that were involved when the Fitzgerald *came apart.*

surge of water in the Soo Lock Canal and popped me like a champagne cork into the wall. To this day, I think the captain of the 1,000-footer did it on purpose because I beat him to the lock."

The captain also says it was unusual to hear of a 10- to 15-year-old ship needing repair work on the keel structure as frequently as that reported on the *Fitzgerald.*

While the report of the Marine Board of Investigation disagrees with Captain Paquette's assertion that a stress fracture in the hull started and ended the chain of events in the loss of the *Edmund Fitzgerald,* a number of sources do lend credibility to his contention and raise questions about the design, construction and maintenance of the ship. In addition to Shannon's analysis quoted above, testimony and statements by several other interested parties constitute a body of circumstantial evidence that a stress fracture could have initiated the disaster – especially in light of Paquette's assertion that Captain McSorley's disregard for weather and his ship handling caused stress on the ship's hull that may have been accumulating through the years and reached a critical stage during the November 10, 1975, storm that sank the ship.

In his *Lake Superior Shipwrecks,* Dr. Julius F. Wolff Jr. devotes considerable space to a discussion of the structural integrity of the *Edmund Fitzgerald,* first citing the testimony of Captain Cooper saying that the ship may have had a stress fracture, "because the water poured into her faster than the pumps could take it out." This speculation is followed by Wolff's examination of the testimony that was cited in Chapter 4 from former *Fitzgerald* Second Mate Richard Orgel. Wolff then invests about 1,000 words to a sizable review of the sworn deposition by George "Red" Burgner, the retired chief steward (cook) who also served as winter ship watcher on the *Fitzgerald* for eight years.[9]

Beyond his earlier cited observations of life when the ship was sailing, it is Burgner's memories from his winter ship-watching duties on the *Fitzgerald* that particularly intrigue Captain Paquette.

"I served as shore captain on Inland boats a winter or two and the ship watchers could be rascals, but the job was kind of lonely, so there wasn't much that went on aboard their boats that they didn't find out about. They were there by themselves a lot of the time, so when work crews were on the boat, it was their chance to shoot the breeze with those workers and keep track of what was being done."

Burgner testified that his winter job convinced him that the ship had a "loose keel" and said he knew that the problem was known to shipyard and company officials and was only partially addressed after a 1973-74 Coast Guard and American Bureau of Shipping inspection in dry dock, when some repairs were made to the keel.[11]

Burgner said that he went with workmen to the ballast tank level below the cargo holds and a shipyard foreman "shoved a crowbar right under it [the keel] and what he pushed out of there was welding rods and everything else [from] when the ship was built. And if that's loose, … the keel would be steady, but the outer hull, it would crack some of the frames and that in the bottom down there. The hull could move."[12]

Burgner said that shipyard workers explained that the welding rods that were pushed from beneath the keel were basically shims used to fill gaps where the hull plating failed to meet solidly with structural members of the keel. The welding rod shimming would then be covered by welding, but the attachment was likely to fail because there was only the width of the rod supporting the weldment.

Burgner testified that patches were made, using plates and bar stock to compensate for gaps between the keel and the shell plating for two sections of the ship's bottom, but not all of the work was finished when the sailing season opened in 1974. Despite that, the ship was apparently certified by the Coast Guard as seaworthy – on condition that the remaining repairs would be completed the following winter. According to Burgner, the work that remained was to continue repairing connections between the keel and the outer shell of the ship – his "loose keel." He was unable to verify if that repair work continued because the ship was laid-up the next winter in Toledo and he was no longer its ship watcher.

He also testified that finding broken welds in the keel area of the ship was difficult because mud from ballast water accumulated there and had to be moved to inspect the keel connection to the hull plating or to do repair work on the keel. Such demudding was not a routine part of ship inspections that he participated in, he said.

In his testimony, Burgner also noted that many of the construction welds were merely "tack welds," as opposed to continuous beads of welding that should have been done during construction of the ship.[13]

From another source ("Faulty Welds Blamed for *Fitzgerald* Wreck," *American Maritime Officer*, November 1976), Wolff quotes August G. Hebel Jr., president of the American Society for Testing Metals, as corroborating Burgner's testimony. Hebel told the professional journal for marine officers that photos of the vessel revealed that there were cracked welds that were not rewelded, but that riveted plates were used to "patch up" the faulty welds. He was quoted as saying, "The hull was just being held together with patching plates." Hebel also stated that most weld failures were due to improper stress relief during construction of the ship – especially with large welds.[14]

That latter bit of information proves interesting when talking with engineers, who say that stress relief is accomplished during welding by either peening (hammering) the weld, in effect expanding it as it cools, or by heating a finished weld to a temperature of 1,200 to 1,400 F and letting it cool slowly. Stress relief is detectable either by the oxidized appearance of a heat-treated weldment or by marks left in the peening process. Of the two stress relief techniques, heat treating is most likely to be used in large welding applications such as those in the keel area of a ship.

Significantly, the engineers say that improper stress relief leads to either cracking of welds or warping of the welded structure.

Finally, the November 10, 1997, edition of the *Star-Tribune* newspaper of Minneapolis, Minnesota, quotes former Second Mate Richard Orgel as saying he believes that the loss of the ship was caused by hull failure, "pure and simple. I detected undue stress in the side tunnels by examining the white enamel paint, which will shatter, crack and splinter when submitted to severe stress." Since Orgel made this observation during his 1972-73 service on the *Fitzgerald* a couple of years before the wreck, it seems to support Paquette's theory that stress may have occurred over a period of time.[15]

While noting that he'd heard a lakes rumor that the 63-year-old McSorley was planning to retire after the 1975 season, Paquette also says that ever since the wreck he's heard that the trip that started on November 9 in Superior, Wisconsin, was scheduled to be the last one that season for the *Fitz* and that the boat was due to return and tie up at Fraser Shipyards for winter work that again included keel repair.

Trevor White, an executive at the shipyards, was unable to find records that verify or refute Paquette's assertion, but does say that it seems unlikely that Columbia Transportation Division of Oglebay Norton Company would have laid up its major ore carrier that early in the season. At that time, White says that Fraser Shipyards was finishing a 96-foot lengthening of Bethlehem Steel Corporation's *Arthur B. Homer*, the sister ship of the *Fitzgerald*, and had also submitted estimates on lengthening the *Fitz* by either 96-feet or 108-feet – something White says has never been mentioned in any previous story about the wreck.

"The companies (owner, Northwestern Mutual Life Insurance Company, and operator, Columbia Transportation Division of Oglebay Norton) were seriously considering that proposal and it's possible that the ship would have tied up here that winter to give us access for planning that work if they decided to go ahead," White says. He notes that the actual work would have had to be done later in 1976-77, because deliveries of the steel required for such projects took several months at that time. No decision had been reached when the ship foundered and, despite Fraser's conversion of Inland Steel's *Wilfred Sykes* into a self-unloading vessel the previous year, White says self-unloading equipment was not included in either the *Homer* or the proposals to lengthen the *Fitzgerald*.

But, while White is skeptical of the rumor that the fatal trip was scheduled to be the last of the season, at least one published article supports Paquette's hearsay. In the July-September 1995 *Anchor News*, the journal of the Wisconsin Maritime Museum in Manitowoc, the late federal judge John W. Peck stated in an article on the wreck: "Dangerous and treacherous the waters of Lake Superior can be, but there was little thought of that as the happy captain and crew (of the *Fitzgerald*) headed for home and fireside at

A frequent winter lay-up site for the Fitzgerald, Fraser Shipyards *in Superior, Wisconsin, had made a proposal to lengthen the ship that was being seriously studied by the owners/operators at the time the ship sank.*

the end of this last trip of the sailing season."[16] Five years after publication, that statement remains unchallenged, although other accounts that were written shortly after the wreck indicated that the ship was scheduled to be laid up a trip or two later in Toledo, Ohio.

"Either way, that would be really early for winter lay-up," Paquette agrees with White's assessment, noting that more common lay-ups at that time were mid- to late January. "By 1975, there was some push for year-round shipping and it was common for ore boats to run on Lake Superior as long as the Army Corps of Engineers could operate the Soo Locks (usually mid-January). I sailed the *Ryerson* in Lake Michigan ice between Escanaba and

Indiana Harbor until January 25, 1975, after the locks closed the season before the wreck, so if the *Fitz* was scheduled to lay up a month to six weeks before the locks shut down, there must have been something wrong with it. Otherwise, why would the company tie up its major money maker? It was unusual to hear that a big, fast ship like that was being pulled from service with way more than a month of a busy shipping season left – unless major work was necessary.

"There was never anything that supported that suspicion in the Marine Board report," Paquette says, "but if the ship did need repair and McSorley chose to sail right into the front of that storm system, then you really have to question his fitness as captain."

The new information revealed by White that the companies were seriously contemplating a major lengthening of the ship raises a further possibility. If they were about to commit the funding to lengthen the *Fitzgerald*, it is possible that some "routine" maintenance work was being deferred because such items would be taken care of as part of the lengthening, which would entail a great deal of work on the hull of the ship.

Pointing to a typewritten sheet, Captain Paquette is reminded of yet another bit of information that raises questions in his mind. "In November 1978, James King, the chairman of the National Transportation Safety Board, traveled with me on the SS *Edward L. Ryerson*. This was after the Coast Guard Board of Investigation and the NTSB had both reached their conclusions. Mr. King told me that he had first asked to take a trip on Bethlehem Steel Corporation's SS *Arthur B. Homer*, but was denied permission. It seemed kind of peculiar to me at the time that a major steel company would refuse the request of the chairman of the NTSB, which had some control over their shipping operations."

His story momentarily veers aside. "Remember that the *Fitz* and *Homer* were sister ships, built by the same shipyard at a time that bridged the construction methods used on the older ore boats and everything that has been built since. For example, welding replaced rivets for many of the joints in the newer ships. I guess I've been suspicious of welded joints ever since my time on a T-2 tanker in World War II. A lot of those ships just broke up in heavy seas when the welds failed. Rivets allow some give in the structure when a ship is flexing and working in heavy seas. Welding is more likely to just break."

Getting back to the story of the NTSB's James King being denied a trip on the *Arthur Homer*, Paquette says, "That made a lot more

LAKE SUPERIOR MARITIME VISITOR CENTER

At the time of the sinking of the Fitzgerald, *its sister ship, the SS* Arthur B. Homer, *was being lengthened by 96 feet at Fraser Shipyards. The lengthened* Homer *operated for five more years, but was ultimately scrapped by Bethlehem Steel Corp.*

sense to me a few years later, when the *Homer* was scrapped just a short while after Bethlehem Steel spent millions of dollars to lengthen her. When that happened, I thought to myself that something about the design and construction of those two ships was suspect."

As already noted by Trevor White of Fraser Shipyards, the *Arthur B. Homer* was lengthened to 825 feet and went back into service in December 1975, immediately after the loss of the *Fitzgerald*. It was laid up in October 1980 – permanently, as it turned out. The ship lay idle for seven years, apparently unwanted by any fleet, and was finally broken for scrap in 1987. Officially, it was reported that retrofitting the ship into a more efficient self-unloading vessel would have resulted in the loss of significant cargo space. By the time it was mothballed, however, the 1980 launch of the *Burns Harbor* gave Bethlehem Steel three 1,000-foot vessels (the others being *Stewart J. Cort*, launched in 1972, and the *Lewis Wilson Foy*, originally launched as the *Burns Harbor* in 1978, and sold to and renamed the *Oglebay Norton* in 1991). Not only did Bethlehem dispose of the lengthened *Homer*, but two other smaller ships, the *Sparrows Point* (also sold to Oglebay Norton in 1991 and renamed the *Buckeye*) and the *Johnstown* were tied up and eventually dropped from Bethlehem's roster of ships.

Paquette gets back to his story of NTSB Chairman King's trip on the *Ryerson*. "I told Mr. King that I had loaded in Superior right after the *Fitz* and sailed in the same storm and was a part of the search fleet. He was a little surprised that I had not been called to testify and was very interested in what I thought happened."

Paquette says that during the two-day trip, he and King discussed many topics, but that the NTSB chairman was most interested in the captain's explanation of what it meant when the Coast Guard and the American Bureau of Shipping allowed ships to increase winter draft by more than 39 inches over several years. When the *Fitzgerald* left Superior on November 9, it was burdened to a draft of 27 feet 2 inches forward and 27 feet 6 inches aft, which was the approved winter draft at that time – but the ship was designed, built and first certified for a winter draft of only 24 feet 6 inches.

"The reason this matters," the captain says, "is because an inch of increased draft on that class boat (Triple A) adds between 110 and 130 gross or long tons (a long ton equals 2,240 pounds, a common nautical weight) of cargo per trip. That means that the 39 inches of additional winter draft allowed the ship to load about 4,300 tons more per trip – an amount of ore that would require something like another trip for every five trips it made at the original winter draft. The increased trip tonnage due to changes in the draft amounted to more than 15 percent of the 26,116 tons of cargo loaded in Superior on November 9."

The 39-inch increase in winter draft was made in three increments, in 1969, 1971 and 1973. Paquette says there was no substantial modification of the superstructure to strengthen ships when they were approved to carry the additional cargo made possible by increased draft. But there is documentation in the Coast Guard report that two of the three years when deeper drafts were authorized, the *Fitzgerald* had repair work done in the area of the keel at the end of the season. Winter repair work on the *Fitzgerald* at Fraser Shipyards in 1969-70 and again in 1973-74 fixed cracks in the welds that fastened the keelson to the hull of the boat.

Captain Paquette says, "The keelson is part of the keel structure, and cracking there would seem to me to indicate that something was happening that the naval designers hadn't taken into account."

The Marine Board report indicates that the 1969-70 repair job involved installing additional vertical stiffeners to the keelson and patching welding cracks, but further cracking developed by the end of the 1973 season, when welding was again required to repair cracking.

National Transportation Safety Board

Washington, D.C. 20594

Office of the
Chairman

November 13, 1978

Dear Captain Paquette:

No one ever enjoyed your hospitality more than I
did. Your thoughtfulness, competence and dedication
were impressive by any standards, but more than anything else I had the feeling I met a real man.

You give us all a sense of pride knowing that
the standards of the "Lakes" are high enough to attract
and keep someone like yourself.

Inland Steel is, indeed, fortunate to have you
working for them and for the Safety Board and the others
committed to our goals to know that you also work for
us.

With every warm wish for the future,

Aloha,

James B. King

Captain Dudley Paquette
Steamer Edward L. Ryerson
#2 Ore Dock Office
Inland Steel Company
3210 Watling Street
East Chicago, Indiana 46312

*National Transportation Safety Board chairman James B. King's letter of
thanks to Captain Paquette for his hospitality and information while aboard
the Ryerson.*

Captain Paquette continues, "Besides the added weight in the
ship's cargo holds, the increased draft also meant that the ship had
39 inches less freeboard, which is the distance from the waterline to
the weather deck where the hatches are located. The ship had been
designed for a winter freeboard of 14 feet 9 inches, but was sailing

in 1975 with only 11 feet 6 inches of structure above water. Naturally, she was much more likely to take waves over her deck. Hell, 12-foot waves would board her in 1975 and that isn't really a huge sea at all. Obviously, the buoyancy and handling were also reduced by the deeper draft, the increased cargo weight and the reduced freeboard."

What had been done to prepare ships for that increased draft? Most of the work addressed mandatory safety items such as placing vertical or horizontal bars over openings in some of the railings and welding lower portholes closed. But, nowhere is mention made of any work to strengthen the structure of the *Fitzgerald* for larger tonnages, less freeboard and deeper draft.

"In my mind, the decision of the Coast Guard and the American Bureau of Shipping to increase the winter draft by more than 3 feet 3 inches with no requirement for strengthening the ship's superstructure seems questionable, at the least. In fact, the first recommendation in the Marine Board report on the wreck was to immediately rescind and review those winter load line increases." They were later rescinded.

He pauses while he pursues a thought, then says, "I can't help wondering if the *Fitz* was maintained to the standards that steel fleet boats were because we would have never sailed if there was reason to believe the ship wasn't in top shape – especially if we thought or were told there was some problem with the keel, which holds the whole ship together."

To understand Captain Paquette's "steel fleet" reference, one needs to know that he differentiates between ships that were owned and operated as part of the integrated supply system of the large steel companies (his "steel fleets") and "transportation fleets," which he describes as "ships for hire" to haul cargo for whatever firm pays the freight bill. Thus, in his lexicon, boats being operated at that time by Bethlehem Steel, Inland Steel and U.S. Steel were steel fleets, whereas Oglebay Norton's Columbia Transportation Division, to which the *Fitzgerald* was chartered, was a transportation fleet. (With the wholesale divestiture of shipping interests by steel makers in recent years, in his view virtually all fleets would be classified as transportation companies today.)

The reason this crops up in his conversation is because the cost of building and operating ships was usually calculated as part of the overall cost of raw materials by the steel companies, whereas transportation fleets were operated on a profit basis and were, therefore, especially sensitive to cost, on-time delivery and maximum tonnages per trip.

Robert Campbell

In peaceful waters and prime appearance in May 1975, a sun-bathed Fitzgerald provided a nearly perfect photograph but gave no clue to its tragic and, likely, violent destiny a few months later.

As a ship that was owned by an insurance company and operated as part of a transportation fleet, was the *Edmund Fitzgerald* especially prone to cost sensitivity during design, construction and later maintenance work? And, if that were the case, was the ship in particular peril in the hands of Captain McSorley, who was known to push his boats to their utmost in all weather conditions?

Captain Dudley Paquette raises these questions because his own experience, training and knowledge led him to conclude that the sinking of the *Fitzgerald* was directly attributable to cracking of the hull as a result of severe stress, at least partly attributable to the bad judgment of her master.

As though supporting Paquette's belief that naval architects and shipyards can make mistakes in design or construction of a ship, the season after the wreck of the *Edmund Fitzgerald* found Paquette making preparations to take out a brand new boat. The circumstances associated with that vessel reinforced his already ample trust in his own instincts as to what is acceptable in a ship – even against the opinions of government inspectors, company inspectors, shipyard supervisors and the designers and builders.

Assigned as master of the *Sykes* early in the 1976 season, Paquette then reported to Sturgeon Bay, Wisconsin, to complete preparations for the launch and sea trials of the self-unloading motor vessel (MV) *Joseph L. Block*, a twin-diesel, 7,000-horsepower, 728-foot-long freighter built to salt-water specifications. Obviously, his reputation with the fleet was skyrocketing, since this ship's construction involved a substantial Inland investment in the future of its materials supply system.

"I didn't like the new design, with no pilothouse or quarters at the bow. It looked like a big barge, but the first time I set foot on that boat is when I really began to dislike it," he says. "I'm not sure what the naval architect was thinking, but when I went up on the weather deck where the hatches are located, I saw immediately that the deck was concave, with no camber to the outside so water would run off. I mentioned it to our company construction supervisor and officials of the shipyard, but nothing was ever reported about it, so I waited until a vice president of the shipyard came aboard and I took a hose and ran water onto the deck while he watched. From four to six inches of water accumulated in the center of the deck at the forward end. By that point, it would have been a huge expense to tear out the deck and redo it, so it's still sailing today with that concave weather deck."

Captain Riley Ward, who has served as a mate and master on the new *Joe Block*, confirms that the deck is "pretty much flat," and agrees with Captain Paquette's account of other details. Meantime, Paquette went back on the *Sykes* until the new *Joe Block* was ready for sea trials in August.

"The new *Joe* had bow and stern thrusters and was really maneuverable," he says. "I moved her out of the shipyard into the channel and backed her through all the curves and turns all the way out into Green Bay (the body of water). A vice president of the company came over and told me it was the most impressive job of ship handling he'd ever seen, but with the thrusters fore and aft to steer with, it was easy.

"We put her through the usual trials with the usual problems – full ahead, full astern, drop anchors (they wouldn't) and the lifeboats wouldn't lift out of the blocks so we could swing them out – but things like that are common during shakedown. The main thing I noticed was that the ship had excessive vibration. A good ship handler is so sensitive to his boat that anything out of the ordinary will wake him out of a sound sleep, so it disturbed me that I just couldn't get a good feel for this boat because of that persistent vibration."

As master on the maiden voyage of the new MV Joseph L. Block, Captain Paquette developed an increasing dislike for the big new ore carrier, characterizing it as being not much more than an efficient barge.

Back at the shipyard, the lifeboat winches were fixed so they'd swing out and workers plugged away at the balky anchors, but when Paquette mentioned the vibration several times, nobody seemed concerned about it. The Coast Guard trial had four officers aboard as he put the ship through her paces – this time with his boatswain and several deckhands stationed in the windlass room with sledge hammers and orders to sledge the anchors down, if they didn't drop. The ship passed the Coast Guard trials, but still had the vibration that he continued complaining about to anybody who'd listen.

Once trials were over, it was time that the new *Joseph Block* start to earn its keep and he ran ore the rest of that season from Escanaba to Indiana Harbor. During that first season, Captain Paquette observed that the new ship was an ore hauling dynamo, although he says it was so cold in the pilothouse during December that the crew needed earmuffs and chopper mittens to stay warm.

"Winter shipping was never very comfortable, but after the diesel powered vessels came along, the crew and the winter ship watchers really took a disliking to them," he recalls. "With steamships, there was almost always comfortable heating everywhere on the ship and the dock would pipe steam to the ship for winter heating, but, obviously, the motor vessels didn't make steam and heating was not very efficient, so you had to put on extra clothes to be comfortable."

He also notes that eight months of sailing resulted in broken oil lines, cracking of the concrete foundation for the steering engine and other damage that he attributed to the vibration, which he had analyzed as a propeller problem.

"The one-year guarantee was up the following August (1977) and I took the new *Joe Block* back to the shipyard to finalize everything. They fixed the items we had recorded, but, when I again complained about the vibration, they told me I was the only one who ever complained about it. I told them there had to be a problem with the propeller. By that time, I had talked so much about something being wrong with the prop that even my chief engineer finally told me he didn't agree with me.

"Anyway, while all of the work to meet the guarantee was being done by the shipyard, I talked with a shipyard vice president and convinced him to have the shipyard check the propeller, since we had the forward ballast tanks filled to raise the stern during the inspection and work. The inspectors for the American Bureau of Shipping brought out a scow, checked the serial numbers on the prop and, sure as hell, the blades were for the thousand-footer the shipyard was building for Interlake Steamship Company."

Smiling, the captain says, "It was really funny how all the company and shipyard guys who had been telling me to shut up about the vibration just disappeared with either red or white faces from embarrassment or fear."

Once that discrepancy was noted and replacement with the proper propeller was scheduled during lay-up the next winter, Paquette headed for Escanaba, where he loaded the 35,000-ton cargo of iron ore that was mentioned in Chapter 1, relying on his weather prediction that winds blowing the length of Lake Michigan would pile water into the Indiana Harbor ship canal and give him the draft needed to get to the dock for unloading.

He smiles and says, "The bottom line on this story is that, even though the new *Joe Block* is a workhorse and should be the pride of the fleet, the deck is still concave and holds water – something the designers and builders or our own company inspectors should have corrected before it got to the point where the work was impossible. But that propeller proved to me that mistakes will be made and, when they are, everybody is so damned busy covering themselves that they don't want to hear any information from anybody who knows what they're talking about.

"I figure if things like that could happen with an expensive new boat in a fleet that prided itself on good ships and good operations, it certainly could happen in other circumstances as well. The only reason it was ever fixed is because I convinced that shipyard vice president that the ship was so shaky that there had to be something wrong."

Harking back to Captain McSorley's reported concern about the "wiggling thing" on the *Fitzgerald*, Paquette says, "If I raised that much of a stink about the vibration, which I knew would not jeopardize the ship or crew, you know I'd have done anything I had to do to find out about something that bothered me that I couldn't figure out."

Was the loss of the ship a star-crossed combination of a hard taskmaster driving a sensitive or compromised ship into the November 10, 1975, storm? The chain of circumstantial evidence would seem to suggest that could have been the case.

CHAPTER SEVEN

"We Are Holding Our Own"

Captain Paquette turns to the window of his summer home overlooking the lake and watches a fishing boat trolling past a rocky island just off his shoreline, then returns to his story of the 1975 storm that sank the *Fitzgerald.*

"Knowing that I'd be in the pilothouse for the duration of this blow, I began to feel a sense of awe and wonder, as my long fascination with weather took over to tell me that this was a night I'd always remember. Here we were, in the middle of the lake, making our way toward the Soo, with wind and barometric readings I had only read about. I had a certain sense of comfort and satisfaction in knowing that my original analysis of the weather system had been right. Even though I had underestimated the severity of the northwest wind and seas that resulted in our present situation, this was definitely a storm that would go down in legends of the Great Lakes and I was in a prime location to record it."

Plowing on, his mate keeping his eyes glued to the radar scope for any information it could provide them, Captain Paquette reflected on past storms and ill winds he'd known, holding fast to whatever would steady him as the SS *Wilfred Sykes* reacted to the massive following seas with an almost hypnotic upward and downward, stern-to-bow motion reminiscent of an intricate dance step.

Occasional checks with the *Blough* assured him that Captain Rolfson, whom he describes as a veteran ship master who taught some of the classes Paquette took in navigation school, also sensed the epic dimensions of the storm. Beyond that, radio reception was patchy until the U.S. Coast Guard Group Sault came on loud and clear to report that the *Edmund Fitzgerald* was reported to be missing and requesting position reports from all other vessels on Lake Superior.

"That first report was that the *Fitz* was last reported near Caribou Island and had requested navigational assistance from the *Arthur M. Anderson*. I reported our position to the Coast Guard, then radioed Neal Rolfson of the *Blough* on another channel and we agreed we would adjust our speed to arrive southeast of Caribou at daybreak to join the search."

As the full impact of that first broadcast began to sink in, the normal quiet of the bridge watch deepened into grim silence. "Each of us just retreated further into our own thoughts, but I couldn't help remembering my words to Lee Ward the night before that they were going to get into trouble."

In following seas at reduced speed, the *Sykes* labored through the darkness, responding with a shudder to each overtaking wave. The normally stable deck of the pilothouse now vibrated, reflecting the power of the wind and seas. The clock ticked slow minutes into hours of travel, yet no bell needed to toll those hours into four-hour watches, for everyone scheduled on watch was standing by well before the hour.

Meanwhile, by 9:25 p.m. the 110-foot U.S. Coast Guard harbor tug *Naugatuck* was ordered to sail to the entrance of Whitefish Bay from Sault Ste. Marie. Because of its size, it was restricted from going onto the open lake until wind speeds dropped below 60 knots. As the *Naugatuck* got under way, an oil line broke and the tug would not actually sail until 9 a.m. on November 11. By that time, the winds had abated enough so the tug could sail in open water and it arrived on the scene at 12:45 p.m. Shortly after 10 p.m., the first aircraft was launched from Traverse City, Michigan, and would be over the wreck site less than an hour later. At 9:30 p.m. on the western tip of Lake Superior, Captain Jimmie Hobaugh and the crew of the 180-foot U.S. Coast Guard buoy tender *Woodrush* rushed to get under way from Duluth, Minnesota, sailing into heavy seas shortly after midnight on November 11, to arrive 22 hours later at the scene shortly after 10 p.m. November 11.

The Coast Guard requested that three upbound foreign salt-water ships, the *Benfri, Nanfri* and *Avafors,* join the search. Sailing west of Whitefish Point on the open seas with massive seas plowing over their bows, the pilots of those vessels refused, saying that the weather made it too dangerous to make the turn to go back to the search area. Responding to a similar Coast Guard request, Captain

Cooper turned the *Arthur M. Anderson* from the long-sought shelter of Whitefish Bay and returned to the suspected area of loss. Captain Donald Erickson took the *William Clay Ford* out of safe anchorage behind Whitefish Point and sailed for the scene. Both ships arrived in the area at about 2 a.m. November 11. In addition, the *Hilda Marjanne*, a Canadian ship, also weighed anchor, but was driven back to the safety of Whitefish Bay by the massive seas.

In the pilothouse of the *Wilfred Sykes*, the radar scope continued spinning its ghostly circular pattern, showing no obstruction to clear sailing ahead. Captain Paquette consulted by radio with Captain Rolfson of the *Blough* and they computed the likely search area by compensating for drift from wind and seas. Their consultation resulted in a heading that would put them in the search area as the search began in earnest at daybreak.

"I kept going back to hearing Captain McSorley tell the *Anderson* the first night of the storm that his boat was working so hard he had reduced his rpms. He'd been captain of that ship for several seasons by then and would have known how it normally reacted in a storm, but he must have sensed something that was more pronounced than he expected.

"I'm convinced that a stress fracture opened at the hinge in the area of the Number 7 ballast tank sometime during the storm and began letting in increasing amounts water for some period before they had any indication of trouble – maybe even the night before, when McSorley told Cooper he was reducing power. If the keel really was loose as the crewmen said, then all that twisting and flexing and bending was putting a terrific amount of stress on the shell plates (of the hull), because the keel wouldn't give them the support it should to stiffen the boat."

Paquette continues, "The Marine Board report says that McSorley told Cooper at about 1400 (2 p.m.) on November 10 that he was 'rolling some' and I can't help wondering why he mentioned that. He was running full ahead in open water between Michipicoten and Caribou islands with no protection from the quartering seas boarding from his starboard stern. Rolling wasn't something you'd have to talk about in those seas – it was natural – so why did McSorley mention it? Was the *Fitz* rolling more than it should? Did he sense something unusual in her motion? That was only an hour or so before he told Cooper about the list (about 3:30 p.m.). I wonder if water inside of her was already causing some difference in the way she handled or felt and McSorley could sense it, but couldn't figure what it was or why it bothered him.

Retired for more than 20 years, Captain Paquette spends summers at his Lake Vermilion home in northern Minnesota, where he has had ample time to reflect on the events leading to the wreck of the Fitzgerald.

"After they passed east of Caribou Island they had the list, of course, and when they left the eastern lee of Caribou they hit huge seas from the starboard (right) stern quarter that were 10 to 15 feet above their weather deck – probably more, if they were settling in the water as I think. Captain Cooper said that he took waves in that area that were 25 to 35 feet. The *Fitz* was certified to sail with only 11 feet 6 inches of freeboard, so the waves were just towering over the weather deck."

McSorley knew that water was leaking into his boat and the list seems to have gotten worse between the time he first mentioned it to the *Anderson* (3:30 p.m.) and 6 p.m., when he told Captain Cedric Woodard, the U.S. pilot on the upbound Scandinavian *Avafors,* that he had a "bad list" and also said he was taking water over his deck "in one of the worst seas I've ever been in."

Captain Woodard knew and had talked with McSorley on the radio many times over the years, but testified that he didn't recognize the voice when the *Fitzgerald* first called for any vessel in the vicinity of Whitefish Point at 4 to 4:30 p.m. and asked the responding Woodard if the Whitefish Point light and radio direction signal was working. After ascertaining that it was McSorley with whom he was talking, Woodard told him neither was working and said later that McSorley sounded strange during the radio conversation.

Paquette analyzes Woodard's contribution to the testimony: "The *Fitzgerald* was taking an increasing list after 1530 (3:30 p.m.), while the crack in the hull opened wider and deeper as the ship worked and twisted in the storm, letting more and more water come aboard. At some point, the fracture invaded the tunnel and probably even the cargo hold as the ship kept pounding and flexing in heavy seas.

"The bad list and big seas that he mentioned to Woodard meant that water was accumulating inside his ship, adding tons and tons of weight to that of the cargo and reducing his freeboard, so he was riding lower and lower in the water. The pilothouse was no longer 35 feet in the air. The waves seemed even bigger than they were because his ship was gradually sinking."

Paquette pauses for a moment, continuing, "Cooper says McSorley reported a starboard list, which would have exposed the ship to even worse conditions than normal. The list would affect the ship's handling and the starboard deck would be lower in the water and exposed to the worst of the northwest seas and wind."

Captain Woodard's later conversation when McSorley mentioned the bad list and big seas was estimated to have taken place only about 2^1/$_2$ hours after McSorley first mentioned his problems to Captain Cooper on the *Anderson*. The officers on that ship told the Marine Board that they didn't believe that the damage was a major concern to McSorley. In fact, they talked several times with him after that and the last thing they heard from him was, "We are holding our own," when they asked how he was making out with his problem. That final transmission from the *Edmund Fitzgerald* was estimated to have taken place at 1910 (7:10 p.m.), with the *Anderson* about 25 miles north-northwest of Whitefish Point and the *Fitzgerald* nine miles ahead and a mile to a mile-and-a-half to the east of the *Anderson's* heading – virtually the exact location where the wreck lies on the bottom.

But as McSorley was talking to the *Avafors* an hour earlier at about 6 p.m., Woodard told the Marine Board that McSorley apparently left the microphone on when he spoke to someone on the bridge, commanding, "Don't allow nobody on deck," and saying something about a vent that Woodard couldn't understand.

Captain Paquette says that such a command goes without saying in such conditions, but raises the question of why McSorley had to emphasize it. The *Fitzgerald* had been in extreme seas for upwards of 20 hours by that point and waves were piling 10 to 15 feet of green water over his main weather deck, so the inadvertent transmission of the command tweaks the imagination.

Virtually a new ship at the time of the Fitzgerald *sinking, the U.S. Steel fleet's giant* Roger Blough, *captained by Neal Rolfson, followed Captain Paquette's* Wilfred Sykes *on a southeast heading through massive following seas that were crashing over their sterns throughout the afternoon and evening of November 10, 1975.*

"Captains try not to reveal very much over the radio because there are a lot of people listening and no captain ever wants to sound like they're not in control. That's probably why McSorley said they were holding their own when he signed off with the *Anderson* just before his ship sank – but his command an hour or so earlier not to let anybody on deck puts a different light on things. For him to say it has to mean that somebody in his pilothouse was willing to risk lives out on the open deck in those seas for some reason – and whoever it was must have believed it was some kind of catastrophe to even consider fighting those seas to fix it."

Asked what would constitute a catastrophe under those circumstances, Paquette says, "It could be any number of things, but it would have to be quite pronounced to see it from the pilothouse after dark in a snow squall. The Marine Board said it might have been some floating object that smashed aboard in the waves and caused damage on the deck or that the spare propeller blade or the hatch crane might have broken loose and caused damage. If I had to guess, I'd say that a forward hatch cover might have washed off, since that would be visible from the pilothouse and I'm pretty sure the covers weren't clamped down with more than a minimum number of clamps.

107

"I'll tell anyone that it was a *monster* sea washing solid water over the deck of every vessel that was out there. The *Fitz* had been slowly sinking for three hours or more, so those huge waves were striking the hatch covers with more and more force and washing more and more water over the weather deck. With that much water coming aboard, any significant opening into the cargo hold would have let hundreds and hundreds of tons of water inside the ship in almost no time."

Since the *Fitzgerald* had been listing for several hours and the pumps apparently had not reduced the list, the entire crew obviously knew that water was somehow getting into the ship – and any further breaching of watertightness would certainly be a cause for alarm. Still, the inadvertent radio transmission of McSorley's command would seem to indicate that his confidence in the ship remained steadfast and that he was unwilling to risk crewmen's lives on the open deck to address whatever had happened.

Meanwhile, Captain Paquette paints a vivid picture of huge seas smashing against, climbing and rolling over the side of the ship, twisting, bending and flexing the hull, creating increasing stress on the already compromised steel shell plates.

"With all that flexing and the extra weight from the water inside her, I think the stern just broke off and capsized from the torque of the steel ripping loose from the rest of the boat. It would undoubtedly sink within minutes. With the stern torn off and all the water inside it, the bow just nosed down, picked up speed and smashed almost straight into the bottom."

Captain Jimmie Hobaugh has a long and, at times, seemingly mystical history with the *Fitzgerald*. The retired Coast Guard officer was on the scene a day after the wreck as commanding officer of the *Woodrush* and, after a Navy airplane reported a large target in the search area on November 14, he and his ship churned through heavy seas with side-scan sonar equipment to locate and gather enough information to identify that target as almost certainly being the *Fitzgerald*. The following spring, he was again on site as commander of the *Woodrush* when the initial videotapes and photos were taken that positively identified the wreckage. Eerily, years later, while escorting a flotilla of ships through the ice in Whitefish Bay, Captain Hobaugh's ship was beset in pack ice that drifted his ship to virtually the exact location of the wreck.

"It seems through all these years that that ship just won't leave me alone," he said during an interview for a profile in the June/July 1998 issue of *Lake Superior Magazine*.

U.S. Steel fleet's Arthur M. Anderson *was giving navigational aid to the* Fitzgerald *and was the last ship to have radar contact with the lost freighter. Captain Cooper reported the loss to the Coast Guard.*

With this background, Captain Hobaugh's interest in the wreck is obvious and intense. Asked about Captain Paquette's assertion that a stress fracture precipitated the wreck, Hobaugh prefaces his comments by saying, "I always tell people that any theory is as good as any other when we're talking about the *Edmund Fitzgerald,* because there aren't any eyewitnesses and there isn't really any way to prove or disprove any idea."

He is deliberately vague about the source, but Hobaugh agrees that water was obviously invading and accumulating in the hull for some period before the foundering, eventually causing the bow to dive into the lake and not recover. With the propeller still turning and a steep angle developing as the bow dove, he says the cargo would begin to shift forward and add to the downward momentum. When the bow slammed into 20 feet or more of muddy bottom, the center cargo section collapsed like tinfoil into the twisted mass of wreckage described by virtually every investigative diving expedition and the stern broke loose. In his version, the rotation of the propeller capsized the intact stern section, while also likely driving it toward the bottom. Hobaugh also says he doubts that hatch covers were washed off, since there do not seem to be any covers missing from the wreck site.

109

While his description does not support or refute Captain Paquette's assertion that the water accumulating in the *Fitzgerald* initially spouted through a stress fracture, Hobaugh's reasoning is nearly word-for-word to that of Captain Paquette when he discusses the likelihood of the ship striking Six-Fathom Shoal near Caribou Island.

And Paquette is adamant on that subject. "Captain Cooper mentioned that he thought the *Fitzgerald* might have hit the shoals north of Caribou Island, but I've never believed that. First, no veteran officer would take a chance close to that shoal in those seas, but the northwest wind and seas on his starboard quarter would also have been drifting him eastward away from the shoals. In fact, Neal Rolfson and I calculated the probable drift from seas and wind as we plotted our heading to the search area and we found the oil slick and flotsam right where we thought we would – well to the east of the normal route from Caribou to Whitefish Bay. The location of the wreck is also to the east of that line, so I've just never believed that he hit the shoals and, as I said, there is no sign of shoaling in photos of the bottom of the stern section or on the rudder and propeller. There should have been scrape marks or pieces missing if the ship hit that shoal hard enough to punch a hole in it. And an earlier search of the shoal by divers didn't find evidence of a recent grounding there."

After the Coast Guard was able to confirm the identity of the *Fitzgerald* with photos taken from a Controlled Underwater Recovery Vehicle (CURV) the following May, some photos of the wreck taken by CURV were published in newspapers later that year.

This author was a guest on Interlake Steamship Company's SS *John Sherwin* when a Detroit newspaper that carried these first published photos of the wreck came aboard at the Soo. Captain William McSweeney and the pilothouse crew somberly and intently scrutinized the grainy black-and-white photos – the most spectacular of which was a brightly illuminated exterior/interior of the pilothouse with what the bridge crew identified as the cord of a radiotelephone drifting outward through one of the smashed windows.

"Not a sign of anybody," First Mate Jim Jacobs said quietly.

"There would have been at least three or four men in there," Captain McSweeney explained to his nautically naive passenger. "Down below, the guys who were off watch would have been in their quarters and were probably trapped there."

By the time the photos were published, the Coast Guard's Marine Board investigation was under way, even though representatives from a number of unions protested that the board's

Captain Jimmie Hobaugh of the U.S. Coast Guard cutter Woodrush *rushed his ship out of Duluth, Minnesota, just after midnight on November 11, facing heavy seas to travel to the vicinity of the wreck.*

findings would be jaundiced by that service's involvement in several areas dealing with marine safety, including licensing, rule changes and the Coast Guard's own preparedness or lack thereof. Nonetheless, the Marine Board spent the better part of 18 months gathering evidence, taking testimony, requesting a wealth of information and writing their report, which met with widespread skepticism in the marine community when it was released.

When the report was completed in July 1977, Gordon Lightfoot's "Wreck of the *Edmund Fitzgerald*" had become not only a national hit recording, but had also introduced the power and fury of Lake Superior's legendary storms to the rest of the world and, undoubtedly, the words he used in describing the wreck have influenced the way that most people think about that disaster. It is worth noting that Lightfoot's lyrics have stood up well through nearly a quarter of a century – as moving and as germane today as when they were first performed. (For words, see Appendix.)

"We just kept sailing along, not really knowing for sure what happened," Captain Paquette says of that period of fragmentary information. "But I kept going back to the first night of the storm and hearing McSorley tell Cooper that the *Fitz* was working so much that he had checked down and was going to try for lee off Isle Royale. I couldn't get that out of my head. Even a slam-bang captain that pushed his boat all the time would be able to tell if something felt different from past storms and it seemed to me that's what I heard in his comment."

In his Marine Board testimony and almost as an afterthought to his commentary about the possible shoaling, Captain Cooper did say that the *Fitz* might have developed a stress fracture that opened a leak and allowed in more water than the pumps could handle.

Captain Paquette states. "To my way of thinking, this ship was a perfect candidate for a stress fracture because she had been subjected for five or six seasons to the strain of hauling cargos that were thousands of tons heavier than she was designed for and had been pounded through all kinds of seas for years. In that same time, she required repairs twice to reattach the hull plating to the keel. There was damage sustained in a grounding and a collision with another ship, as well as three instances when she struck lock walls at the Soo and had to lay-up for repair. Put all of that together with McSorley's reputation for running in all weather and full speed ahead and it seems to me a stress fracture would be the first thing that would come to mind.

"And remember, McSorley was running full ahead right up to the time he reported to Cooper that his boat had developed a list after he passed Caribou. Only then did he check down his speed so the *Anderson* would be able to close up a little. A half hour or so after that, he reported that his radars weren't working and asked the *Anderson* to provide navigational assistance to make his way to Whitefish Bay through the storm and snow squalls. That seems to show that he had radar when he navigated the Six-Fathom Shoal area and would have missed it easily."

* * *

While his analysis that the *Fitzgerald* suffered a stress fracture is theoretical, Captain Paquette has first-hand experience with a stress fracture on a ship that he says was a much less likely candidate than the *Fitzgerald* for this particular problem.

In 1978, he was named captain of the SS *Edward L. Ryerson,* which was the flagship of the Inland fleet and marked him as the captain that the fleet now trusted with the company's most important guests. During his vacation that summer, he received a call from the fleet office that the *Ryerson* was tied up in Duluth with a crack in the hull and that the crew was unable to find the last Certificate of Inspection, which the Coast Guard required to be displayed in a prominent location.

"I told the office it was right where it should be, in a frame next to the door of the captain's office, but they told me to catch a plane and get to Duluth to take over. Sure enough, we found the certificate in the frame by my door and I went down to have a look at the damage to the hull.

"I'd heard of stress fractures, of course. Everybody who sails has heard about ships that developed cracks in their hulls, but I didn't have any experience with one because I had enough training and common sense to stay out of trouble and check down the rpms if I didn't like the way the boat was working. I also knew there'd been some fairly heavy weather on the trip up to Duluth and heard later from a couple of the crew that the relief captain pushed the ship pretty hard in those seas.

"Anyway, this crack was nowhere near as serious as what (he suspects) happened on the *Fitz,* but I was still shocked when I saw how deep it went into that beautiful ship and how much water it leaked. Luckily, the chief engineer had spotted water dripping around the rivets as he was putting out the gangplank and he went back down and found the crack. Our pumps were able to handle the volume of water without difficulty, but the thought of water getting into my ship just made me mad. That wasn't going to help anything, though, and I made arrangements to take her to Fraser Shipyards in Superior, Wisconsin, and they got us fixed up and back out for the end of the season.

"It wasn't a hazard to the *Ryerson* or the crew because the crack was discovered fairly early while the boat was empty and tied up, but the amount of damage, the volume of water coming in through the crack and the fact that I knew the boat had been maintained to the highest standards and had never really been abused all told me

113

that this was not a boat you'd expect to develop a stress crack. The fact that it did just confirmed my original thinking that a stress fracture sank the *Fitz*. The *Ryerson* had been in service a year longer than the *Fitz* was when it sank. I've never had any reason in anything I've heard or seen since then to change my mind. If it could happen to the *Ryerson*, it could sure the hell happen with a boat that was always pushed hard and sailed in all kinds of weather."

* * *

In testimony, the officers of the *Anderson* estimated the distance they trailed the *Fitzgerald* at 17 miles at about 3:30 p.m., when McSorley first told them of the problems on the *Fitzgerald* and indicated that he'd check down his speed to allow the *Anderson* to close up. By 7 p.m., $3\frac{1}{2}$ hours later, the distance between the two boats had closed to about nine to 10 miles. Since the *Anderson* was turning for its top speed of 14.6 miles per hour and made up about seven miles between them, the *Fitzgerald* was only making about 12 mph in that $3\frac{1}{2}$-hour time span – four to five miles an hour below its normal speed of 16.3 mph and two to three mph slower than the *Anderson*.

At that reduced speed, the quartering seas boarding from starboard quarter would be striking the ship with greater force and rushing farther forward than would have been true if the ship were proceeding at full speed. The weight of that topside water, added to that of the water that Paquette believes was accumulating in the ship's internal spaces, spelled doom when the already damaged and listing ship left the eastern lee of Caribou Island and discovered even bigger waves and harsher northwesterly winds in the open sea between Caribou and Whitefish Point.

Captain Cooper told the Marine Board that the northwest seas built to 25 feet or more when he was 10 miles southeast and out of the lee of the island. Captain Paquette agrees with that estimate, saying, "At that time, I was on the open sea, but taking those seas directly over the stern of the *Sykes* and, as I said, they were so massive that they washed over the boat deck – that's the highest deck at the stern, about 22 feet above the waterline – and were meeting midships. I had green water, the center of the waves, washing right to the front of my weather deck.

"I can only imagine what it must have been like with those huge waves coming aboard from a quartering angle. Every wave would be pounding and twisting and bending the ship, working the hinge unmercifully and ripping the stress fracture wider and wider, deeper and deeper."

THE TIMES

Home Newspaper of the Calumet Region

Hammond—East Chicago, Indiana; Calumet City—Lansing, Illinois; Tuesday, November 11, 1975   4 Sections—36 Pages—

The Edmund Fitzgerald, which disappeared off radar scopes almost without warning amid mountainous waves on Lake Superior.

Ore Carrier Sinks; 29 Lost

Headlines in newspapers like this one from Calumet City, a suburb of Chicago, Illinois, startled the world with news of the Great Lakes disaster that seemed nearly impossible in the modern age of shipping.

His eyes have drifted far to sea during the observation and now refocus on the chart before him, as his finger traces the 140-degree heading that the *Anderson* had been monitoring and reporting to the *Fitzgerald*.

Asked if he thinks Captain McSorley ever understood the grave nature of the situation before the wreck, Captain Paquette pauses a moment and says, "I think he believed he was going to make Whitefish Bay and as captain he had to convey confidence to his crew. But he had to know he had serious problems and he had checked down his speed. If he ever seriously thought that the ship was going down, I think he'd have said something to either the *Anderson* or the *Avafors* when he talked with them.

"By this time in the whole thing, McSorley had really run out of options. The course he was on put him at the mercy of those northwest seas, and he really didn't have any room to run before the seas like the *Blough* and I were doing in the open lake. There was maybe an hour or less of running room to his southeast and, in snow squalls without radar, if he tried that he'd have no way of knowing what was ahead or where he was, and that area of the lake is full of shoals."

The finger taps the chart at the spot where the wreck lies on the bottom of Lake Superior. "You can see from this location that the seas probably drifted him to the left of his heading, because he's a mile or two to the east of the 140 degree route into Whitefish Bay from Caribou. Of course, the light and radio direction signal at Whitefish Point were both out that night and he was in snow squalls without his radars, so the only navigational aid that McSorley had was his gyrocompass and the radar fixes the *Anderson* passed along to him. He was listing badly and had checked down his speed, which would affect his helm, there was water in his hull that would make the ship sluggish and he had no choice but to keep running for the shelter of Whitefish Bay.

"The ship was filling with water through that crack, the pumps couldn't keep up and he was obviously going down by the bow – in fact, the entire ship was no doubt settling deeper and deeper. Whenever that crack first penetrated the inside of the boat, by 1730 or 1800 (5:30-6 p.m.) he reported the 'bad list' to Captain (Cedric) Woodard on the *Avafors* and said he was in the worst seas he'd ever seen. He was taking those huge seas completely over his weather deck and, if they were running with just a minimum number of hatch clamps dogged down, those boarding waves could have pounded hatch covers off and allowed the waves to wash directly into the holds. If most of the hatch cover clamps weren't dogged down, what does that say about his concern for the weather advisories – or about the Coast Guard's conclusion that the cause of the wreck was ineffective hatch closures? To my way of thinking, the fact that most of the hatch clamps that can be seen in photos are not distorted or damaged indicates that they were not clamped down in the first place. The ship was not seaworthy in that storm. If that were the case, the Coast Guard's conclusion would have to change from ineffective closure to indifferent closure – which I'd say would fit into most definitions of negligence."

CHAPTER EIGHT

All Hands Lost

Having spent longer than is comfortable sitting, talking and answering questions, Captain Paquette rises out of his recliner and stands before one of the large picture windows at his expansive lake home in northeastern Minnesota. Its view of Lake Vermilion's islanded surface is unimpeded from 50 feet above the rippling blue surface and, just on the eve of the 25th year after the wreck of the *Edmund Fitzgerald*, the captain reflects on the aftermath of the disaster.

"As we entered the search area about 0300 (3 a.m. on November 11), intermittent snow gave us a glimpse now and then of the Coast Guard aircraft engaged in their search of the area. One of the aircraft had a huge spotlight (described in the Marine Report as a 3.8 million candle power xenon-arc "Night Gun") that lit up the whole area under it.

"All of us in the pilothouse agreed that the crews on the aircraft were displaying devotion to duty and courage we had never seen before, with winds that had to be really bouncing them around.

"By daybreak, we were southeast of Caribou and logged our position and winds of 28 knots, but slowly diminishing. The *Blough* was nearby and both of us were in a huge oil slick. We advised the Coast Guard that we were in the midst of a pool of fuel oil that likely came from the *Edmund Fitzgerald*.

"We continued on our course, looking for any sign of survivors and silently saluted the *Anderson*, which was making her way toward us. We knew from monitoring the radio and the Coast

Guard's reports that Captain Cooper and his crew had been giving the *Fitzgerald* navigational help and had alerted the Soo of the disappearance. They had taken a helluva beating out on the open lake for 36 hours, but now deserted safe anchorage in Whitefish Bay to come back out and help in the search and rescue efforts – but that was really the only decision a professional mariner can make when there might be survivors that need assistance.

"Debris of all kinds – mattresses and personal gear that ranged from life jackets to insulated gloves – slowly floated by us. Every damned piece that came into sight during the search promised to be a survivor or at least a body, but when we'd get closer we'd see that it was just more junk floating in the oil. In our search passes we spotted and picked up all kinds of stuff. The *Blough* even recovered an inflated life raft, but there wasn't any sign of survivors.

"We made a pass through the search area and, after talking with the Coast Guard and with Neal Rolfson on the *Blough*, we agreed to reverse course and make another pass to look for survivors, although I think we were all pretty well convinced that the length of time since the disappearance and the severity of the wind and waves in that cold water made this effort nearly fruitless. Still, we had to try.

"Reversing course was a challenge, since there was still significant west-northwest seas. We warned the crew to brace for heavy seas, swung into our turn and at least half our weather deck was submerged at one point. Once around, I told everyone to be on the lookout, since miracles can happen.

"We continued through the search area and each minute made it less likely we'd find anyone alive – but where the hell were the bodies? Surely, some of the crew would have gotten into life jackets and some of them must have escaped as the ship foundered. Where the hell were they?

"Of course, we never found anyone. Eventually, using extreme care, I worked my way down through the shoals all the way to Ile Parisienne. The Coast Guard finally released us from the search effort at 1300 hours (1 p.m.). As we departed the search area, the seas and the winds were just negligible and I felt comfortable in going down to my cabin, but I couldn't relax.

"Somewhere very close to where we had been sailing, that great boat that we'd all come to know as the Big *Fitz* had to be laying on the bottom and not one damned sign of the crew. How could such a ship and its whole crew just disappear? The *Fitz* was bigger, had more horsepower and was 10 years newer than the ship I was on.

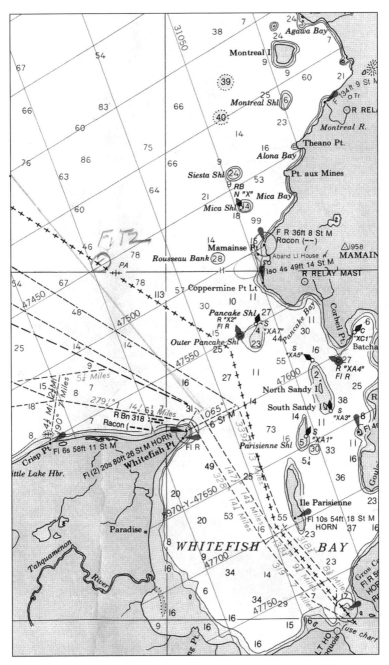

The Edmund Fitzgerald *disappeared from the radar screen at 7:30 p.m. in Canadian waters near Whitefish Point, Michigan, on November 10, 1975.*

How the hell could this big, powerful, almost new vessel just drop out of sight? And why didn't any of us hear a distress call?

"I couldn't get it out of my mind. We may work for different companies and compete with one another to be first into or out of a port or the Soo Locks, but the men who work the Great Lakes boats are a pretty close-knit bunch and I knew that I might even recognize some of the names of crewmen when they were announced. Some might even be friends from navigation school. Where the hell were those guys?"

Captain Paquette kept going over what little he knew, wondering why there had been no distress call. By that time, ships had several radio units, some using battery power, so even the loss of ship's power to the pilothouse wouldn't shut them down. Even the *Carl D. Bradley* had time to make a couple of emergency calls when the ship suddenly broke up and went down in the 1958 Lake Michigan storm, so what could happen so suddenly that no one in the *Fitzgerald* pilothouse had a chance to grab the microphone and call a Mayday?

"It seemed clear to me that they had to have either capsized very quickly or something caused the bow to suddenly dive under, since every other possibility I could think of would allow the watch in the pilothouse time to send some kind of distress call – which several of us should have heard.

"There had to have been some kind of hellish chaos going on. As I said earlier, the pilothouse usually gets quiet during times of stress, but what about a calamity? Would that final instant when the water crashed in through the windows cause panic to the watch? I had no way of knowing for sure, but thought back a few hours, when I sensed fear for the first time in my own pilothouse."

Later, he would discard the idea of capsizing and he enumerates his thoughts on that subject.

"Even with water inside her, that still wouldn't make capsizing very likely. I'd say it's barely possible that such a massive amount of water could have accumulated in one side of her that she turned belly up, but it's not as likely as the bow and stern either breaking apart and sinking suddenly or so much water accumulating in the bow that it dove deep into a wave and couldn't recover."

He turns from the window and explains his reasoning. "Taconite pellets are very stable cargo and just don't move around in big seas like that sloppy ore that we had on the old *Joe Block* back in 1950. Once you finish loading and trimming the boat, you can forget about cargo shifting and causing the ship to turn over and

COMMANDER, NINTH COAST GUARD DISTRICT
CLEVELAND, OHIO 44199

copies To Captain D J Paquette
for Posting on
Bulletin Boards

JAN 27 1976

Mr. R. O'Brien
Fleet Manager
Inland Steel Company
30 W. Monroe Street
Chicago, Illinois 60603

Dear Mr. O'Brien:

On 10 November 1975 when the Steamer Edmund FITZGERALD sank in
eastern Lake Superior during a violent storm, the search for
survivors involved a number of vessels and aircraft. The Steamer
Wilfred SYKES was one of those vessels.

The officers and men of the SYKES are to be commended for their
efforts devoted to trying to save mariners in distress under very
treacherous lake conditions. Their professional response, though
fruitless, was undoubtedly appreciated by the relatives and
friends of the seamen and most assuredly is appreciated by us.

I deeply regret that neither we nor anyone were able to help, but
it is truly warming to note the response of the other Great Lakes
mariners under such hazardous and tragic circumstances.

Please convey a most sincere "Thanks" to Captain Pacquette and
his crew.

Sincerely,

J. S. GRACEY
Rear Admiral, U. S. Coast Guard

*Letters of commendation were issued to the fleet offices of ships that
participated in the search effort mounted by the Coast Guard after the loss
of the* Fitzgerald.

you don't have to worry about the cargo having any adverse effect
on your handling," he analyzes. "Also, a load of taconite pellets has
a low center of gravity in a boat because they're so heavy (130 to
140 pounds per cubic foot, depending on moisture content). That
cargo provides a lot of ballast that would tend to keep a boat right
side up, but, if the boat did roll over, that whole cargo would slam
down onto the hatch covers and rip them off. The hatch clamps

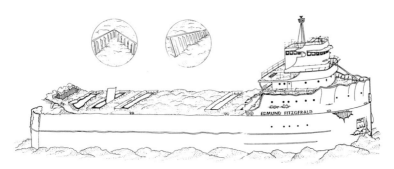

Drawings of the wreck contained in the Coast Guard Board of Investigation Report show the severed bow section of the Fitzgerald sitting upright in about 30 feet of mud more than 500 feet below the surface.

would be completely distorted or torn off and the covers would sink. The cargo would spill to the bottom with them. We know from the photos that almost none of the visible hatch clamps showed distortion.

"If the cargo spilled out of the hold, the *Fitz* might have even continued to float, because the loss of the cargo would have lightened her by 26,000 tons and she might have had enough buoyancy left to stay up, even if she was upside down.

"When the drawings of the wreck site were published, they showed that at least some of the hatch covers still seem to be in place. There is actually a hatch cover inside the Number 6 hatch, which wouldn't happen if she had capsized, but might if the bow dunked under and the hatch cover was pushed into the hold or if the bow went down so fast that the hatch cover came down behind it and landed in the hatch.

"And if she turned over and sank suddenly, the wreckage would be on top of the hatch covers and pellets, but in the drawings and the photos I saw at Harbor Branch Oceanographic Institution in Ft. Pierce, Florida, there are pellets scattered all over the bow section, so capsizing just doesn't add up.

"Maybe most convincing, though, were the pictures in Ft. Pierce of the *Fitz's* bow, with the stem (a heavy upright steel beam) at the bow of the boat bent around almost to a right angle. To distort that steel like that, the bow had to have dived into the bottom very hard – in other words, the bow section smashed into the bottom pretty much head on, then settled into the upright position we see it in today."

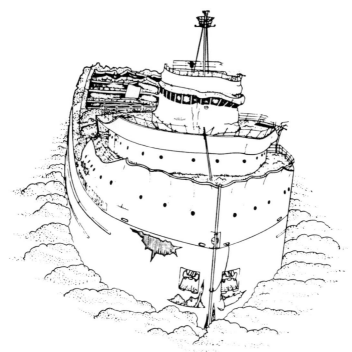

Enormous damage to the bow section is evident in the Coast Guard drawings and illustrates the forces at work as the big ore carrier plowed downward into the lake bottom.

* * *

With a myriad of questions running through his mind and exhausted from having had almost no sleep in 48 hours, Paquette returned to the pilothouse to take the ship through the Soo Locks and continue his journey to Indiana Harbor, where the attorneys representing the *Fitz*'s owner company embarked and debarked in relatively short order, after he told them he felt negligence was the cause of the wreck.

After all these years, the questions keep nagging at him.

"I've never gotten the wreck out of my mind and I kept coming back to the question of why McSorley and Cooper disregarded the very clear weather forecasts radioed to all of us on a regular basis for many hours before the storm actually struck? They were only about two hours ahead of me, so they were facing the same weather and had the same reports I did. They could easily have ducked onto the north shore and would have avoided the worst of the pounding like

The inverted, intact stern section of the Fitzgerald *has been closely examined by several of the deep diving expeditions, with little or no evidence of grounding or shoaling on the bottom, rudder or propeller.*

I did – even if they decided to do it after the gale and storm warnings were broadcast in the late afternoon and evening of November 9. As I said earlier, a few hours of extra sailing time wouldn't ruin their season and the *Fitz* might have survived, if they had just heeded the forecasts and taken the more protected route up the north shore and then crossed Lake Superior with northwest, following seas and wind."

Queried as to whether he's ever been in a situation where his own safety and that of his crew were jeopardized, Captain Paquette surprisingly skips over the storm he's been describing and looks back to an episode seven years earlier in his career as a ship master.

"Early in the 1968 season, the third season I was captain of the old *Joseph Block,* we were loading ore at Escanaba, Michigan, when I got a telephone call from the fleet office that my neighbor, friend and former chief engineer on the *E.J. Block* had died and his wife was requesting that I serve as a pallbearer at his funeral."

His orders from the fleet were to finish loading and run the *Joe Block* back to Indiana Harbor and debark there for the funeral. The

U.S. COAST GUARD

first mate was temporarily promoted to captain while Paquette was absent.

"At 0400 (4 a.m.) the day of the funeral, I got a call from the fleet office that Old *Joe* was aground at the Porte Des Morts (Death's Door) entrance from Lake Michigan into Green Bay (the body of water). They told me the company's King Air airplane was waiting to fly me up over the ship so I could look over the situation from the air and would drop me at the Sturgeon Bay (Wisconsin) Airport to catch a Coast Guard boat out to the ship."

Captain Riley Ward, who was a mate on the ship at that time, remembers the incident vividly. "I had gotten off watch about three hours before and was asleep, when all of a sudden the damnedest rumbling and shaking was going on after the bow of the boat just jerked up. The rumbling seemed to go on forever and I hit the deck in a helluva hurry. When I got up on deck, it was clear that we had hit something pretty hard and that there had to be serious damage to the ship. I also saw that we were out of the channel and had to have hit one of the reefs that are all around Death's Door."

Captain Paquette picks up the story. "When I flew over the Old *Joe*, it was obvious they were well up on a reef, but the water to the north looked to be good. When I finally got out there and went up the rope ladder to the deck, the first mate that was serving as captain met me at the rail and he was just beside himself.

* * *

"We looked the situation over, then went up on the bridge. I had already made up my mind that the good water to the north was our only chance to get her off the rocks. A tug was on the way from

125

Sturgeon Bay and, while we waited for it to get out there, we sounded the ballast tanks to see how badly we were damaged. The after tank under the engine room was flooded, but my chief engineer thought our pumps could handle that. We also found water in our Number 1 port ballast tank near the bow – which we figured was where the ship first struck the rocks.

"Anyway, sometime later, the Roen tug *Arrow* arrived from Sturgeon Bay and it was only maybe a 50-tonner. As he sailed around our stern, the tug captain reported that at least a third of our propeller was out of the water. I looked things over and talked with the tug captain, who told me he'd do whatever he could to help us get the ship to the north, where the good water was.

"I consulted with my chief engineer and he didn't want to use our engine for fear of damaging the prop or the engine. I told him to forget about that, because the ship would either be a junker or a monument if we couldn't work it off the rocks. The chief agreed to give me what power he could and I ordered everyone into life jackets, with all unnecessary personnel on deck and the lifeboats dropped out over the side so they'd be ready if needed.

"We didn't know if we could move her or not, or even if she'd float if we did manage to get her off the rocks. The only people below decks were the chief engineer, one assistant and a fireman in the engine room, and they had orders to get out of there in a helluva hurry, if I sounded the general alarm.

"We tied up with the tug at our stern and his orders were to put strain to the north to see if we got any movement at all. If we did, I had told him to keep inching us toward that clear water and we'd add our own power to try and help. Sure enough, when that stern line tightened, we could feel it inching around. I signalled the tug to keep up the tension and rang my engine room to give me full reverse power. The chief gave it everything it had and slowly we started to move back off that reef and came free in good water, although we took a definite port list as we came loose."

Captain Ward chuckles and reinforces the comment about the list. "I'd call it a little more than just a port list," he says. "That boat was seriously tipping to port and there were a few seconds when we weren't sure if she was going to stabilize or just roll on over. Luckily, it settled down, but was really listing to port."

With the pumps for the ballast tank under the engine room and the Number 1 port tank on full, the list abated somewhat and the engineer told him they seemed to be holding their own, although the ship continued its left-hand tilt.

THE DOOR COUNTY ADVOCATE

ESTABLISHED BY JOSEPH HARRIS, SR. ON MARCH 22, 1862   SERVING STURGEON BAY AND DOOR COUNTY SINCE 1862

VOL. 107 – NO. 18   TWO SECTIONS, 24 PAGES   STURGEON BAY, WIS. 54235 – THURSDAY, MAY 23, 1968   CIRCULATION 7349   **PRICE 10¢**

THE STEAMER Joseph Block ran aground off Europe bay early Wednesday morning and was freed late Wednesday afternoon. The Roen tug Arrow pulled on the ship. The Block was able to proceed to Manitowoc under her own power. She will be drydocked for damage inspection.
—Harmann

Tug frees grounded ship

Joseph Block Damaged in 'Door' Mishap

The 549 ft. Inland Steel ore carrier Joseph Block was freed from the bottom off the tip of Door county Wednesday afternoon at 4:30, 12 hours after she went aground.

The vessel was out of Indiana Harbor, traveling light to Escanaba for a load of ore. She grounded in 12 ft. water, 3/4 mile southeast of the outer shoal buoy off Plum Island. No reason has been given for the ship's being in that position.

An inquiry will be conducted by the Coast Guard Marine Inspection office in Milwaukee. The ship will be drydocked at Manitowoc for assessment of damages and repairs. Dry docking is mandatory after a grounding.

One of the ship's forward holds took on water in the incident but the vessel was able to proceed to Manitowoc under her own power after she was freed. The Coast Guard cutter Woodbine accompanied her.

The Block has a crew of 32 and carrying capacity of 11,500 tons. She was two hours out of Escanaba when the mishap occurred.

Shipping company officials summoned the Roen Steamship Co. tug Arrow to the scene from her home port of Sturgeon Bay. Between the Arrow and use of the Block's own engines the big freighter was worked free.

Water was too shallow for the Woodbine to get in. A Coast Guard boat from Plum Island was going to run a towing hawser from the Block to the Woodbine but meanwhile the ship was freed.

The Woodbine arrived on the scene early in the afternoon. Her home port is Grand Haven, Mich.

The grounding of the old Joseph Block *on a reef at Porte Des Morts entry to Green Bay while Captain Paquette was on funeral leave provided the most dramatic "close call" in his 30-year career as a fleet officer.*

"I knew we couldn't pussyfoot around out there, so I gave orders to sail immediately for the shipyard at Manitowoc, about 60 miles to the south.

"As we started down the Wisconsin shoreline of Lake Michigan, a Coast Guard cutter stayed with us and followed us all the way in. We were all in life jackets and we kept the lifeboats swung out because there was no way to tell if or when we might start to break up or capsize. That trip seemed endless, even though we were running as fast as we could. The ship was shaking like hell and that just added to everybody's nervousness, because vibration almost always means trouble.

"We called ahead that we needed to have the dry dock available and the shipyard said it would take a while because they'd have to move a Coast Guard cutter – I think it was the *Mackinaw* – to make the blocks available for us. Well ahead of time, we also called an emergency request that the two bridges over the waterway be opened because I was bringing the ship in really brisk. Those bridges were up quite awhile and created a real traffic jam in town, but I got Old *Joe* to a dock and tied up, where it again took a heavy list after the pumps shut down. After we got her into dry dock, we went down with the yard supervisor and looked Old *Joe* over. I just couldn't believe the amount of damage – something like 90 plates were stove in. I still wonder how the hell we stayed afloat, but the fact that we did is one reason I still feel good when I think of the Old *Joe*."

Captain Ward agrees. "There was a lot of damage all right. Looking back even today, it seems impossible that we could make that trip with so much of the bottom pounded out of it."

Once their part of that harrowing adventure was over, it was up to the company to make a decision to either fix the ship or not. The fleet office decided not to repair it, but the Steinbrenner Kinsman Lines Inc. bought the ship, had repairs done and ran it for several more years.

With this experience as background, when he's asked what his best guess is about the final minutes in the *Fitzgerald* pilothouse and what may have been going on in the minds of the men there, Captain Paquette's mind drifts back over his 32 years of sailing experiences.

"I'm not a guy who lets his imagination get the better of him, but whatever happened in those last seconds had to have been very sudden and terrible. The ship had been listing and was pitching and rolling for hours already in seas that were breaking over the

128

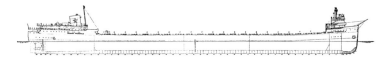

U.S. COAST GUARD

As outlined by Captain Paquette's rationale, the Fitzgerald cracked open just forward of the rear superstructure, allowing water inside the ship and ultimately leading to the break-up of the ship.

starboard and rushing forward over the deck. For a long time, everyone had been hanging onto any fixed object near them just to stay upright and in one position. More and more water was accumulating inside the hull and was probably adding to the motion of the ship, causing the bow to dig deeper and deeper into the waves. All of that action would be twisting and flexing the hinge area, working the metal like a kid bending a wire back and forth until it snaps.

"In the end, the hinge area finally did snap and the stern broke loose. The torque (a rotating or twisting effect) from the propeller and the metal breaking flipped the stern over. It would flood immediately and begin to go down. The electric lines to the forward area would be severed when the stern came loose and the remaining 500 feet or so of the forward section would have been whipping and churning from the force of the stern ripping off, creating total chaos. The bow was already down from all of the water in the hull and within seconds more water would rush in. The bow section would be completely waterlogged and just nose down. As the bow dove into the lake, the cargo would begin moving forward from the downward incline, adding to the momentum and would just explode anything in its path when the bow slammed into the bottom.

"From the moment the stern came loose, the whole orientation of the ship was totally unstable. Everybody was tossed around like rag dolls and nobody would be able to hold onto anything to steady himself. They were probably grabbing for anything to stop their own motion, but there was no way anybody could have gotten to a battery operated radio or hold on long enough to make a May Day call. In less than two minutes from start to finish, the stern broke off and sank, the bow nosed in, picked up momentum as it went down and then hit the bottom with a terrific impact. The water quickly caved in the pilothouse windows as the bow started down, but surely not before everybody in the pilothouse who was still conscious would know it was the end."

His focus comes to rest on a white-tailed deer that regularly visits his lakeshore property late in the day to sample the browse in his back yard. The change of scene accompanies a minor adjustment in his thought pattern.

"Most people eventually ask me why McSorley didn't mention any of his troubles to the Coast Guard. After all, he called them at 4:30 p.m. to ask if the Whitefish Point radio beacon and light were working and he had already told the *Anderson* about the list and damage on his deck and told the *Avafors* pretty much the same thing an hour or so after he talked with the Coast Guard, so why not let the Coast Guard know?"

He pauses to be sure of his words. "To be honest, I think McSorley was like a lot of us who didn't want them to know very much, because the Coast Guard was pretty much in a position where all they could do was make trouble for us. Most of us figured they were in cahoots with the Lake Carriers' Association when they wrote the rules and regulations for sailing, certified the officers and the seaworthiness of ships and all their other duties.

"But how would the Coast Guard help him, anyway? He'd already been told that they couldn't even keep their light and radio beacon working at Whitefish Point – so why tell them about something they might be able to use against him in the future? They didn't have a single vessel available in the area that was ready to sail in those seas, but, even if they did, all of us knew that anything they sent out would be too small to be of much assistance to an ore boat, so what difference would it have made if they knew about his troubles? Even if a cutter had been able to sail, it wouldn't help very much, so why tell them about something they might be able to use to make trouble for him later?"

He pauses, then reiterates his earlier statement. "But I think the real reason that McSorley didn't say anything to them is because he figured that he was going to make it into Whitefish Bay – probably right up to the moment when the water smashed through the pilothouse windows."

Noting there are a number of factors that keep recurring about the wreck, he turns his attention to the captain first.

He's convinced that Captain McSorley believed the *Fitzgerald* was so big and powerful that he could push the ship through any storm. But Captain Paquette says that 7,000 or more horsepower pushing the ship full speed ahead in seas reported at various times on November 10 as being from 12 to 35 feet caused critical stress to the ship's hull – which, according to Chief Steward George

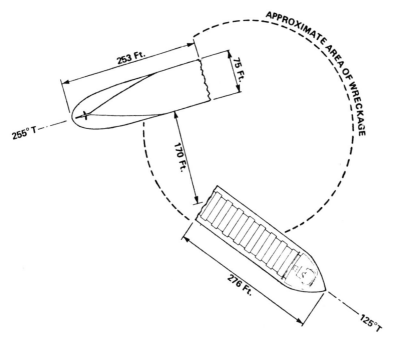

APPROXIMATE AREA OF WRECKAGE

253 Ft.

75 Ft.

255° T

170 Ft.

276 Ft.

125°T

U.S. COAST GUARD

The intact bow and stern sections at the shipwreck site lie in a mass of wreckage and taconite pellets that constituted the center holds of the Fitzgerald.

Burgner's sworn testimony, McSorley had been told was not securely fastened to the keel by crewmen working in the bottom of the ship earlier that summer.

Saying that a captain is responsible for everything aboard his ship, from basic safety to fresh linens for guest quarters, Paquette says, "You really have to fight against anything that might distract you from your duty – which is the well-being of the ship and everybody on it. The chief steward (Burgner) said that McSorley was worried about his sick wife and was just waiting for his retirement. He also said that McSorley wouldn't push the crew to keep up with regular maintenance work and, if that wasn't being done, was anything of a more serious nature not getting his full attention? I can understand thinking about your family and naturally there are times when you have worries about them – but it isn't going to help anybody if you're so worried that it gets in the way of your judgment and you wreck your boat or someone is hurt or killed because of your inattention. If he wasn't able to concentrate completely, was he doing his job as well as he should? If not, then it's time to step down or get out."

But, perhaps because he was so conscious of it, Captain Paquette's attention keeps coming back to weather. "It was obvious to me as we listened to their conversations (the captains of the *Anderson* and *Fitzgerald*) Sunday afternoon (November 9) that neither of them had been keeping track of the low pressure system. Captain Cooper said in Jim Marshall's *Shipwrecks of Lake Superior* that he only started keeping a chart after gale warnings went up later in the afternoon (6 p.m.). (See Capt. Cooper's letter, Appendix B, page 157) [17]

"I doubt that McSorley even bothered to start then, because he just didn't sound worried about the weather – which was still nice. By then, starting a chart wouldn't give them much of a picture because they didn't have the background information on what the system had been doing or what it might turn into. Captain Cooper even said that when they did plot the Weather Service information, it just looked like 'normal November low pressure' – but if he'd been charting it as long as I had, he should have known otherwise and would have gone up the north shore with me. If the two of us were on the north shore, I think McSorley might have decided to stay with us and he would have saved his ship from the worst of the beating it took out on the open lake. Anyway, is it negligence at the command level to ignore information that the Weather Service regularly broadcast for many hours before the storm developed?

"Then, what about the former mate's (Richard Orgel) testimony that the ship had an odd motion that scared McSorley? If he was worried about the way the ship acted, why didn't he demand to know what caused it? Surely, as captain, he knew the ship had needed keel repairs at least twice? And, if his crew came up from below and told him the keel was 'loose again' the summer before she sank, wouldn't you think he would check it out and, if it was loose, demand to have it fixed? If he ignored a problem with the keel and sailed into a storm, I think you have to call it 'negligence.'

"Since the captain's primary responsibility is the safety and seaworthiness of his ship, it seems to me to spell negligence to ignore something about his ship that made him uncomfortable."

He sits back down in his recliner and gazes upward at the sturdy log trusses of the interior roofline of his lake home.

"I can't help wondering if the Marine Board ever heard anybody say that McSorley was famous as a heavy-weather captain who pushed his ship into weather that most masters would try to avoid – which was well-known among sailors.

RUS HURT

This dramatic shipboard photo of the weather deck and stern of the Irving S. Olds *shows the twisting effect that a ship experiences in heavy weather. Although common, such action creates stress on the metal plating of a ship.*

"Of course, McSorley wasn't the only captain that sailed in that storm. The *Anderson*, the *Blough* and we on the *Wilfred Sykes* sailed through it and several other ships that were a lot older and less powerful than our boats also caught some of the heavy weather and survived. We were all doing what we were paid to do – which is to get the cargo to its destination."

But, while his *Sykes* and the *Blough* were sailing southeast, with seas coming directly at their sterns – the most advantageous heading they could have sailed for that particular trip – he says that the *Fitzgerald* and *Anderson* were sailing a much more problematic route that subjected the ships to greater stress in the monstrous seas.

Not surprisingly, the unions representing shipboard personnel raised several objections when the Marine Board was set up, saying that a board set up by the Coast Guard would produce a biased report, since the officers on that board would be passing judgment on things that the Coast Guard was involved in – things like inspecting and certifying lifesaving equipment, certifying the ship, five-year dry-dock inspections, the annual inspections, the spar deck inspection that was done on October 31 – only a couple of weeks before the ship went down – and the search and rescue effort conducted by the Coast Guard after the *Fitzgerald* sank. Despite those objections, the Coast Guard went ahead and set up the Marine Board to investigate the wreck.

Of their report, Captain Paquette says, "Some people have praised the Marine Board for doing a good job of criticizing the Coast Guard's own part in the events surrounding the accident, but what did they come up with as their explanation of the wreck? They dismissed a stress fracture. They dismissed shoaling. They pretty well down played the Coast Guard record that the *Fitz* needed repairs at least twice (the winter lay-ups of 1969-70 and 1973-74) to fix broken welds fastening the outer shell to the keel.

"Their own official report says under the 'History and Maintenance' section that a crack in the port gunwale was also discovered in 1969-70, caused by a 'fault in the original construction of the vessel' – the same year cracks in welds were first found in the keelson area and repair work was done. More cracks in the keel area were also repaired in 1973. A small crack in a gunwale probably wasn't a big deal, but this boat was only 10 or 11 years old in 1969, when they found the first keel problem and that flaw in construction. Those broken welds in the keel area would seem to me to be a clear indicator of design or construction problems. Wouldn't you think the board might have been a little suspicious of an almost new boat when they heard about those cracked welds in the keel area, especially when a crack in a gunwale was caused by a flaw in construction?

"Also, the cook and ship watcher (George Burgner, in his deposition) said he knew that McSorley and an official of Oglebay Norton knew the ship had a loose keel, but he said that after the accident the company lawyers told him to stay out of sight down in Texas and to just lay low and say nothing."

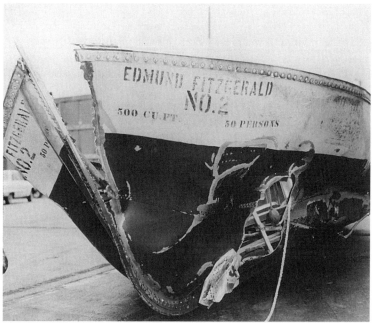

This badly damaged lifeboat shows the savagery of the forces that tore it from its davits and set it adrift as the big freighter plunged for the bottom. The lifeboat was later recovered by ships searching in the wreck area and is on display in Sault Ste. Marie.

Since the *Fitzgerald* had been weather-beaten for years in all kinds of seas, Captain Paquette says that stress on the hull from earlier trips likely contributed to the eventual failure and reiterates the fact that during the six years before the ship sank there had been three cargo tonnage increases that totaled some 4,290 long tons per trip more in 1975 than the ship was designed and certified to haul when launched in 1959. On November 10, the *Fitz* was loaded 3¼ feet deeper than its original winter load line, with each inch of additional draft adding 110 to 130 tons of additional cargo.

In addition to a history of repairs to the keel structure, there is the report of former Second Mate Richard Orgel telling of undue stress he observed in the side tunnels and the unusual action of the boat in moderately heavy seas, which Burgner's sworn statement also noted.

"I've never seen any indication that the Marine Board ever heard from anybody who knew anything about the actual design and construction of the *Fitzgerald*. Did they ever hear testimony from welding experts to see what they might have to say about cracks in structural welds that were only 10 years old? Why isn't there testimony in their report from somebody at the shipyard that worked on the ship or from the winter ship watchers to see what they knew about repairs?"

As a final defense of his theory that a stress fracture sank the ship, Paquette ticks off the four ships most intensely involved in the brunt of the November 10, 1975, storm. "The *Blough* was a brand new ship, only in its second or third season, so the bugs were out of her and she was as strong as a ship can be. My *Wilfred Sykes* had spent the entire previous winter and spring in the shipyard for retrofitting as a self-unloader and had a whale of a lot of new steel inside her that really stiffened her and made her feel like a new ship. The *Anderson* had undergone lengthening by 120 feet the winter before the trip, with all of the hull modifications and additional new steel involved in that process.

"So, of the four of us traveling through the worst of the storm, the *Fitzgerald* was the only ship without new steel in her hull. She had been pushed through bad weather many times through the years and was also a ship with a record of the hull breaking loose from the keel. If all of that doesn't add up to the probability of some kind of hull failure, then I don't know a thing about ships and ship handling – and those are the first things I'm likely to brag about.

"The Marine Board's report came out and said that water getting into the cargo hold through 'ineffective hatch closures' or, maybe, a collision with some floating object caused the wreck. Based on their finding, they issued recommendations to address the problems that they thought existed. The very first one was to rescind the amendments in Load Line Regulations, which increased the draft – or reduced a ship's free board and buoyancy – by 39 inches from what the *Fitz* was designed and built for.

"That was the one recommendation that made sense – but the Coast Guard was the agency that authorized those load line changes in the first place, so what are we supposed to think about their part in that whole thing?"

The Marine Board also made several recommendations having to do with the hatch cover clamps, vent repairs and maintenance and evaluation of the hatch closures, while also recommending that Coast Guard ships that would be involved in search and rescue should be in good repair and available during bad weather months on the Great Lakes.

"But the Coast Guard has been in charge of marine safety since it was first formed (in 1915), so where were they when all of those patented hatch covers were installed and used on ships during all those years? And didn't they know about a couple of hundred years of history that show that November and December are bad weather months when ships are lost on the Great Lakes and their own ships ought to be available for assistance? Why was there only one Coast Guard ship that was able to sail on the open seas of Lake Superior that night and that one located way over at the other end of the lake (the USCG buoy tender *Woodrush* in Duluth)? Their two vessels anywhere close to the east end of the lake that could have handled those seas (the *Mackinaw* at Cheboygen and *Sundew* at Charlevoix, both at the north end of Lake Michigan) were both tied up in repair status. Of course, as I said, anything they'd have sent wouldn't have been much good to the *Fitz* at that point in those huge seas.

"The Marine Board also recommended development and installation of better survival gear on the boats and better lifesaving training for crews and several other things that had always been under their jurisdiction and should have been done years before, if the recommendations were worth anything.

"The facts are that the Coast Guard licensed the captain, inspected and certified the ship and they authorized decreasing the winter freeboard by more than 39 inches, which increased the cargo tonnage by more than 4,000 tons above what the *Fitz* was designed and built to haul.

"Did the Coast Guard have any responsibility in the accident? Not if hatch cover closures were so ineffective that they let in enough water to sink her, as the Marine Board said. They surely didn't, if there was a navigational error and the ship hit a shoal and was damaged, as the Lake Carriers' Association said. Even if the captain beat up his ship and exercised bad judgement, as I say, it would only be the Coast Guard's responsibility if somebody brought charges and proved that the captain deliberately damaged the boat or was incompetent – which never came up and never became an issue.

"Since the wreck was more than 500 feet under water and the crew were all dead, there was no way the Coast Guard and the LCA could investigate if the ship had a problem, but it was easier and a lot cleaner for them to blame the wreck on ineffective hatch cover closures or a shoaling. The LCA's idea of a shoaling leaves everybody pretty well free of blame, since the storm was so fierce that the officers on the ship could have been disoriented."

He shifts the recliner into a laid back position and muses, "I don't think that any of the questions we had 25 years ago have gone away. It seems like every time we get a new piece of information, it just muddies things up.

"For example, one of the early dives found the port pilothouse hatchway open, with the dogging latches open. Does that mean that someone in the pilothouse suspected trouble and undogged the door to provide an escape route on the lee side of the ship? How would we ever know?

"Then the 1994 diving expedition (Frederick Shannon, Expedition '94) found a body in a life jacket near the wreck and you'd naturally expect that it would be from the *Fitz*, but (historian Frederick) Stonehouse saw the videotape and says the life vest is an older type than those that were on the boat, so where did the body come from and what's it doing next to the wreck? Short of recovering the body, which nobody wants to do, it's just one more mystery about the *Fitz*.

"As I said before, the starboard list they took off Caribou Island would have exposed the deck to the worst of the northwest seas and wind. I know how big the seas were where I was sailing, because we took water over our stern so hard it broke a strongback on one of the lifeboats on our boat deck. Cooper said he took seas that put water on the bridge deck – 35 feet above the water line."

He pauses. "We'll never know what was going on when the U.S. pilot (Capt. Cedric Woodard on the Swedish ship *Avafors*) said he overheard McSorley's order not to let anybody out on the deck, but if he actually said it, there had to have been something that a mate wanted to get control of. The National Transportation Safety Board said that waves may have stove in or washed off hatch covers and it certainly could have happened on a ship that was already listing into those huge seas – we just won't ever be sure.

"But my experience with that crack in the *Edward L. Ryerson* and everything else I learned in 32 years of sailing indicates to me that the ship sprung a leak from the stress on her hull during that storm. The seas that cracked the *Ryerson* were a helluva lot smaller than what he was in and he just kept pushing that ship full speed ahead for nearly 20 hours in conditions that were severely twisting and bending the hull. Then, too, there is quite a bit of evidence that the ship had some hull problems and there is also a question if it may have even needed repair when that trip started."

He tilts his chair forward and his eyes again take in the pile of documents, books and reports on the coffee table in front of him. He looks up and says, "After 25 years of mystery, what do you call it when the Coast Guard's official report pretty well admits that lowering the winter draft lines by more than 39 inches over five years was probably questionable? Or you have a captain that loads right to those load lines and pushes his ship hard in every possible way, says the ship has a 'wiggling thing' that scares him, but there is no evidence he ever tried to have it checked or fixed? Or a captain that ignores very clear weather advisories and sails right into the front of a November storm? And you have a ship that Coast Guard records show had keel repair work at least twice in five years – a ship that is loaded every trip for years with thousands of tons more cargo than her design called for? Then you have a winter ship watcher who says he knows that a company official was told that the ship had a loose keel and also testified that he heard deckhands tell the captain that the keel was loose again during the season she sank? And why was he told by company lawyers and officers to just stay in Texas and not talk to anyone about the wreck?

"What do you call it when all of these questions are about a ship that is only 18 years old, but in just the last six years had been damaged by grounding, a collision with another ship and several collisions with lock walls?

"I don't know what you call it, but the word that still comes to my mind 25 years after that ship sank is: Negligence!"

Epilogue

F ree for two decades of the all-consuming responsibility of being a Great Lakes ore boat captain, Captain Dudley Paquette has traveled at will from his spacious summer home on Lake Vermilion in northern Minnesota to Florida and from the American Southwest to overseas destinations, but the *Edmund Fitzgerald* tragedy occupies a strangely enduring place in the back of his mind, even though subsequent events in his life have provided personal challenges and, in one instance, nearly ended his life.

Stretching to his full height, he says, "I really believe that building this cabin probably saved me from being a cripple for the rest of my life. When I was planning my retirement, I bought this land and planned to put a cottage on it for a summer place – maybe something like 30 by 40 feet. After I retired, I went piloting on foreign vessels for 50-some days until I damned near got killed when I was going down a ladder that gave way beneath me and I fell 20 feet or more onto a steel deck. I was all smashed up, but I was finally able to hobble around after months in hospitals and physical therapy, so I came up here and worked like hell peeling and putting up the 868 cedar logs in this place. It was tough, but that's how I regained my strength and I swear it's why I'm able to get around so well today."

Turning from the lake scene, he delves backward into this stage of his life. "I told Inland Steel in the spring of 1980 that I was retiring, and the fleet office couldn't believe it. I was only in my early 50s and could have sailed for another 13 or 14 seasons if I wanted to, but I'd had enough of walking on that tightrope.

"I mentioned before that a captain not only has the constant pressure of command and is always on duty, but every detail about the boat is your responsibility. You also have to keep the guests entertained and be sure you don't irritate anybody from the company who could wreck your career. By that time, the fleet management was changing from experienced transportation people to what we called office boys. Some of them were so green, you'd have to explain port and starboard to them two or three times. Then, you're away from your home and family for long periods of time during the season and when the season is over you just want to get away and relax – but the off-seasons had gotten pretty short by that time, so a month or two after you laid your boat up you had to start getting ready for the next season.

"Anyway, by 1977 or 1978, I definitely knew I was taking my pension as soon as I was eligible – and the rules had changed to allow retirement after 30 years of service and your age didn't matter, so I told the company in 1980 that I wanted my pension.

"I was still young and had an unlimited license to pilot boats anywhere on the Great Lakes, so I signed up with the Western Great Lakes Pilots Association to pilot foreign ships coming into the lakes. In fact, I was right up at the top of their seniority board and caught my first assignment within a couple of days of leaving Inland Steel. I worked pretty much anytime I wanted to until the accident early in the season."

"Piloting was a lot different from working the ore boats," he says. "Every boat had different handling and the crews spoke different languages, so you could never be sure they really understood what you were saying. We were responsible at our end for taking the ship from western Lake Superior down through the Soo Locks and St. Marys River to whatever point another pilot relieved us. It was sort of a tramp's life. For example, on the few trips I got in, I took a brand new Norwegian boat up to Marathon, Ontario, for a load of paper, then went to Thunder Bay to pilot an English ship with a crew from India through the Soo, caught a Japanese ship for Thunder Bay, piloted another trip through the Soo and picked up an upbound German ship, then went back to pilot the Japanese ship downbound from Thunder Bay."

His grin indicates that this transient lifestyle as a pilot agreed with him. He especially remembers leaving Thunder Bay on the bridge of the Japanese freighter, when one of the ship's officers inquired about their position.

"I'd been in and out of that port so many times for Inland that I knew it like the back of my hand, so I just opened the sliding door near me, stuck my head out and sniffed the breeze and put my finger on the chart," he laughs. "I told them that we were right where I was pointing and the young officer that challenged me took a bearing and I was right on the money. After that, it got to be a joke, and somebody on the bridge crew was always asking me to sniff the breeze to find out where we were. It was a lot of fun."

The fun ended at Port Huron, Michigan, 56 days into his new career when a ladder he was using to depart from a Yugoslav ship gave way beneath him. Falling headfirst about 20 feet, he was fortunate that a seaman on the deck of the pilot boat below him threw up his arms to protect himself and hit him in the head. The blow was enough to change the orientation of his fall and, instead of landing head-first, he slammed onto the metal deck of the pilot boat on his right side, crushing bones in his leg, arm and shoulder and suffering massive injuries.

"I was just lucky that the Sheriff's Department was searching nearby for a woman who had fallen off a sailboat and got involved immediately. They rushed me to a hospital in Detroit and I didn't wake up until the day after the accident. I kept telling everybody I'd be out of there in a day or so – until a lady doctor handed me a mirror and I saw how beat up I looked. I spent five weeks in the Detroit hospital, then the rest of the summer and autumn I was in several hospitals in Minnesota recuperating and doing therapy. Even when I was discharged, I was in tough shape and not much good to anybody. I went to Florida for the winter and worked my therapy there, then came up here (Lake Vermilion) the next spring to work on this place. I peeled the logs for the first 42 feet of this place by hand with a drawknife. It was hard work and hurt like hell most of the time. I had very little strength in my hand and arm and I was limping around on gimpy legs, but I kept at it and the size of the cabin just kept growing as I got stronger.

"By the time I felt like I had gotten my strength back, the cabin was 160 feet long, with my quarters here on this end and guest quarters in a completely self-contained unit down at the other end. It's a great arrangement for when my daughters and sons visit with their families or when I have other guests because it gives them privacy, but we're all under one roof. The only way in here is by boat and that's fine – it keeps me on the water and reminds me that that's where I earned my living and got enough time to earn my retirement.

Retired for more than 20 years from the rigors and responsibility of captaining an ore carrier, Captain Paquette takes full advantage of sunny days at his 160-foot summer home on Lake Vermilion in northern Minnesota.

"Anyway, all the grunt work on this place gave me a lot of time to think about all the things that I learned during the years I sailed and, now and then, I'd remember how helpless we felt sailing through all the junk in that oil slick over the *Fitz,* hoping to find survivors."

As autumn leaves turn color in northern Minnesota, he transfers his residency to Las Vegas, Nevada, where he and son Dan own and operate a travel company that regularly uses the social skills and tact he developed as a captain in 16 years of dealing with important guests to host parties of guests on golfing and other tour excursions.

"For me, there is an endless fascination with the night the *Fitz* went down. I was out there and I know what it was like. It will never leave me."

DEPARTMENT OF TRANSPORTATION
UNITED STATES COAST GUARD
16732/S.S. *Edmund Fitzgerald*
15 April 1977

From: Marine Board of Investigation
To: Commandant (G-MMI)
Subj: S.S. *Edmund Fitzgerald*, O.N. 277437; sinking in Lake
Superior on 10 November 1975, with loss of life

Conclusions

1. Preface. The SS *Edmund Fitzgerald* left Superior, WI, on the afternoon of 9
November, 1975 en route, Detroit, MI, with a full cargo of taconite pellets.
That evening, and the next day, *Fitzgerald* proceeded eastward in Lake
Superior, on a course north of the charted lanes due to the weather, heading
towards Whitefish Bay and the Locks at Sault Ste. Marie, MI. At the same
time, a severe November storm was crossing Lake Superior and, as a result,
Fitzgerald encountered worsening weather throughout the early hours of the
10th of November, and by that afternoon, was experiencing winds in excess of
50 knots and seas approaching 16 feet. At approximately 1530 (3:30 p.m.) 10
November, *Fitzgerald* reported damage, but did not, at that time or in
subsequent communications, indicate that it was of a serious nature or that
there was any immediate concern for the safety of the vessel. No distress
message was received. *Fitzgerald* sank sometime after 1910 (7:10 p.m.) 10
November, 1975, at a position 46° 59.9'N, 85° 06.6W, approximately 17
miles from the entrance to Whitefish Bay, MI.

There were no survivors and no witnesses to the casualty. Information
available to the Marine Board consists of testimony of people who were on

board other vessels in the area at the time *Fitzgerald* was lost, of people who had served on *Fitzgerald* prior to its last voyage, of employees of the company which operated the vessel, of other persons familiar with the vessel or similar vessels or its cargo, of personnel of the Coast Guard and of the American Bureau of Shipping who had conducted inspections and surveys on the vessel, of Coast Guard personnel who participated in the extensive search which followed the report of its loss, of personnel from the National Weather Service concerning weather at the time of the loss, of personnel at the facility where the vessel loaded its last cargo, and of information from the several underwater surveys which were conducted on the wreckage which was found on the bottom of Lake Superior.

Information available is incomplete and inconsistent in the following particulars:

a. Position. The only information available on the position and trackline of *Fitzgerald* is in the weather reports sent by *Fitzgerald* and in testimony of the Master and Watch Officers of the SS *Arthur M. Anderson*, which was following *Fitzgerald*, in voice communication with it, and observing it visually and on radar. The weather reports from *Fitzgerald* scheduled at 1300 and 1900, (1:00 and 7:00 p.m. respectively), 10 November, were not received.

The position of *Fitzgerald* relative to that of *Anderson* cannot be reconstructed. Information available is based on the recollections of the Master and Watch Officers on *Anderson*, since the relative position of *Fitzgerald* was observed intermittently on the radar, but not recorded. Testimony on these observations is inconsistent. For example, the officer on watch on *Anderson* recalled that *Fitzgerald* was "a shade to the right of dead ahead," as *Fitzgerald* passed northeast of Caribou Island, while the Master thought it was a point to point and a half to the right at that time.

The Master and the Watch Officers on *Anderson* testified at length as to the position and trackline of *Anderson* in the afternoon and evening of 10 November. An analysis of this testimony shows that the vessel was navigated by radar ranges and bearings, that, at times, positions were determined but not logged, that course changes were made without simultaneous determination of position, that positions were determined as much as 20 minutes from the time that course changes were made, and that the courses steered varied from the course logged because of expected drift. The Marine Board attempted to reconstruct the trackline of *Anderson* and found that in order for the vessel to have steered the courses and have been at the positions at the times testified to, the speed of the vessel would have varied from a low of 5 mph to a high of 66 mph. But the Master testified, and the engineering log confirmed, that throughout the period, *Anderson* maintained a steady speed, turning for 14.6 mph. Accordingly, it is concluded that the times and positions reported by officers of *Anderson* were not sufficiently accurate to allow the trackline of either *Fitzgerald* or *Anderson* to be reconstructed.

b. Difficulties Reported by *Fitzgerald*. *Fitzgerald* reported the loss of two vents and some fence rail, indicating that topside damage had occurred to the vessel. The flooding which could be expected to result from the loss of any two tank or tunnel vents would not be serious enough, by itself, to cause the loss of the vessel.

Fitzgerald reported, at the same time, that it had developed a list. The existence of the list which would result from flooding of any two ballast tanks, a tunnel, or a tunnel and a ballast tank would not, of itself, indicate damage sufficiently serious to cause the loss of the vessel.

Fitzgerald reported that steps were being taken to deal with the flooding and the list, and that two pumps ("both of them") were being used. *Fitzgerald* had four 7,000-gpm pumps and two 2,000-gpm pumps available, indicating that the flooding was evaluated by personnel on board *Fitzgerald* as not sufficiently serious to create a danger of loss of the vessel.

Fitzgerald reported difficulties with its radars, and requested *Anderson* to provide navigational information.

Fitzgerald reported slowing down to allow *Anderson* to catch up. This action might have been taken because the Master of *Fitzgerald* knew or sensed that his problems were of a more serious nature than reported to *Anderson*.

c. Underwater Survey. The underwater survey showed that mud covered a majority of the wreckage, that the midships section of the hull was completely disrupted, and that the stern section was inverted. Movement of the survey vehicle disturbed the mud, which limited visibility and made it difficult to survey individual components of the wreckage. However, the survey provided the Marine Board valuable information with respect to the vessel's final condition and orientation.

2. In the absence of more definite information concerning the nature and extent of the difficulties reported and of problems other than those which were reported, and in the absence of any survivors or witnesses, the proximate cause of the loss of the SS *Edmund Fitzgerald* cannot be determined.

3. The most probable cause of the sinking of the SS *Edmund Fitzgerald* was the loss of buoyancy and stability which resulted from massive flooding of the cargo hold. The flooding of the cargo hold took place through ineffective hatch closures as boarding seas rolled along the Spar Deck. The flooding, which began early on the 10th of November, progressed during the worsening weather and sea conditions and increased in volume as the vessel lost effective freeboard, finally resulting in such a loss of buoyancy and stability that the vessel plunged in the heavy seas.

4. The following factors contributed to the loss of *Fitzgerald*:

a. The winter load line assigned to *Fitzgerald* under the changes to the Load Line Regulations in 1969, 1971 and 1973 allowed 3 feet, 3¼ inches less minimum freeboard than had been allowed when the vessel was built in 1958. This overall reduction in required freeboard also reflected a reduction in Winter Penalty for Great Lakes vessels. Not only did the reduction in minimum required freeboard significantly reduce the vessel's buoyancy, but it resulted in a significantly increased frequency and force of boarding seas in the storm *Fitzgerald* encountered on 10 November. This, in turn, resulted in an increased quantity of water flooding through loosely dogged hatches and through openings from topside damage.

b.The system of hatch coamings, gaskets, covers and clamps installed on *Fitzgerald* required continuing maintenance and repair, both from routine wear because of the frequent removal and replacement of the covers and from damage which regularly occurred during cargo transfer. That the required maintenance was not regularly performed is indicated by the fact that the crew of the vessel had no positive guidelines, in the form of Company requirements or otherwise, concerning such maintenance. That the required repairs were not regularly performed as damage occurred is indicated by the fact that significant repairs had been required during the previous winter lay-up period and by the fact that more repairs of the same nature were expected, since a general item to repair hatch covers and coamings had been included in the work list for the winter lay-up which *Fitzgerald* was approaching when it was lost. It is concluded that the system of cargo hatch coamings, gaskets, covers and clamps which was installed on *Fitzgerald* and the manner in which this system was maintained did not provide an effective means of preventing the penetration of water into the ship in any sea condition, as required by Coast Guard Regulations.

c. Whether all the cargo hatch clamps were properly fastened cannot be determined. In the opinion of the Marine Board, if the clamps had been properly fastened, any damage, disruption or dislocation of the hatch covers would have resulted in damage to or distortion of the clamps. But, the underwater survey showed that only a few of the clamps were damaged. It is concluded that these clamps were the only ones, of those seen, which were properly fastened to the covers and that there were too few of these and too many unfastened or loosely fastened clamps to provide an effective closure of the hatches.

d. The cargo hold was not fitted with a system of sounding tubes or other devices to detect the presence of flooding water. It is not known whether any efforts were made to determine if water was entering the cargo hold. If the hold had been checked at a time when the level of water was below the cargo surface, the extent of flooding could not have been determined. It is inconceivable that flooding water in the cargo hold could have reached a height to be seen, without a seasoned Master taking more positive steps for vessel and crew safety than were reported. Therefore, it is concluded that the flooding of the cargo hold was not detected.

e. The cargo hold was not fitted with transverse watertight bulkheads. As a result, the flooding water which entered could migrate throughout the hold, extending the effect of the flooding and aggravating any trim which existed.

5. At sometime prior to 1530 (3:30 p.m.) on 10 November, *Fitzgerald* experienced damage of sufficient magnitude to cause the Master to report topside damage and a list. Significantly, the Master of the *Fitzgerald* reported the damage rather than the incident which caused it. It is the opinion of the Marine Board that the incident, while possibly of a serious nature, was not of such extent as to have caused, by itself, the loss of the vessel and, further, that

148

the full extent of the incident was not perceived by vessel personnel. The Master noted the list and topside damage and incorrectly concluded that the topside damage was the only source of flooding. He began what he believed were adequate, corrective measures – pumping spaces which would receive flooding from damaged vents – and thus felt the problems were under control.

The topside damage could have been caused by the vessel striking a floating object which was then brought aboard in the heavy seas. This also could have resulted in undetected damage opening the hull plating above or below the waterline and additional unreported damage to topside fittings, including hatch covers and clamps. Intake of water into the tunnel or into one or more ballast tanks through the damaged vents and open hull would have produced the reported list and increased the rate of cargo hold flooding. The most likely area of damage would have been in the forward part of the ship. The vessel had entered a snow storm approximately one-half hour before the topside damage was reported. In addition, *Fitzgerald*'s radars were reported inoperative shortly after the damage was reported, and may have been malfunctioning for some period before the report. Both the reduced visibility from the snow storm and the radar malfunction would, in the opinion of the Marine Board, have reduced the likelihood that the crew of the vessel could have detected the object in sufficient time to take effective action to avoid it.

The topside damage could have been caused by some unidentified object on board breaking away in the heavy seas. Flooding through such damage could have caused a list. While there were objects on deck which might have come adrift and knocked off a vent cap or damaged a hatch coaming, the only items on deck which had enough mass to do sufficient damage to the hull to cause a sustained list were a hatch cover, the hatch cover crane, or the spare propeller blade. If such extensive damage had occurred, a seasoned Master would have reported it. Such a report was not received.

The topside damage and list could have been caused by a light grounding or near grounding on the shoals north of Caribou Island. Although the testimony is not fully consistent, both the Master and the Watch Officer on *Anderson* indicated that *Fitzgerald* passed within a few miles of Caribou Island and that they had a conversation concerning the closeness of *Fitzgerald* to the shoals north of the island. It is considered possible that a light grounding or near grounding on these shoals could have occurred. The vessel could have been damaged from the grounding, from the effect of the violent seas which would be expected near the shoals, or from the shuddering that the vessel would have experienced as it passed near the shoals. The damage could have been on deck, below the water line, or both, leading to the reported topside damage and list. The Marine Board is unable to reconstruct the trackline of *Fitzgerald* south of Michipicoten Island, however, *Fitzgerald* was observed to pass two to three miles off Michipicoten Island West End Light from which position a single course change to 141 degrees T would have taken the vessel directly to Whitefish Point on a track well clear of the shoal areas off the northern tip of Caribou. Had there been a delay in making the course change after passing Michipicoten, *Fitzgerald* would have passed closer to the shoals. But, the distance between Michipicoten and the shoals is such that it appears that a delay in making that course change of upwards of an hour would have been required to cause *Fitzgerald* to have actually reached the shoals.

The list could have been caused by a localized hull structural failure, resulting in the flooding of a ballast tank or tanks. There is no correlation between such an occurrence and the reported loss of vents and fence rail. The survey of those parts of the wreckage which could be seen showed no evidence of brittle fracture.

The Marine Board concludes that the exact cause of the damage reported cannot be determined, but that the most likely cause was the striking of a floating object.

6. In the opinion of the Marine Board, the flooding from the damage reported, and from other damage which was not detected, most likely occurred in the forward part of the vessel, resulting in trim down by the bow. By the time the damage was reported by *Fitzgerald*, the flooding of the cargo hold had reached such an extent that the cargo was saturated and loose water existed in the hold. Because of the trim by the bow, this water migrated forward through the non-watertight screen bulkheads which separated the cargo holds, further aggravating the trim and increasing the rate of flooding.

7. Because there were neither witnesses nor survivors and because of the complexity of the hull wreckage, the actual, final sequence of events culminating in the sinking of the *Fitzgerald* cannot be determined. Whatever the sequence, however, it is evident that the end was so rapid and catastrophic that there was no time to warn the crew, to attempt to launch lifeboats or life rafts, to don life jackets, or even to make a distress call.

Throughout November 10th the vessel was subjected to deteriorating weather and an increasing quantity of water on deck. With each wave that came aboard, water found its way into the cargo hold through the hatches. As the vessel lost freeboard because of this flooding and as the sea conditions worsened, the frequency and force of the boarding seas increased, and so did the flooding. The Master of the vessel reported that he was in one of the worst seas he had ever seen. It is possible that, at the time he reported this, *Fitzgerald* had lost so much freeboard from the flooding of the cargo hold that the effect of the sea was much greater than he would have ordinarily experienced. Finally, as the storm reached its peak intensity, so much freeboard was lost that the bow pitched down and dove into a wall of water and the vessel was unable to recover. Within a matter of seconds, the cargo rushed forward, the bow plowed into the bottom of the lake, and the midships structure disintegrated, allowing the submerged stern section, now emptied of cargo, to roll over and override the other structure, finally coming to rest upside-down atop the disintegrated middle portion of the ship.

Alternatively, it is possible that *Fitzgerald* sank as a result of a structural failure on the surface, resulting from the increased loading of the flooding water. However, this is considered less likely because such a failure would have severed the vessel into two sections on the surface, and one or the other, if not both sections would have floated for a short while. With the weather conditions that existed at the time *Fitzgerald* was lost and, in particular, with the winds in excess of 50 knots, if either or both of the pieces had floated for any time, significant drifting would have occurred. But the survey of the wreckage showed that the two main pieces were within a ship length, thus little or no drifting took place.

8. There is no evidence that the crew of *Fitzgerald* made any attempt to use any lifesaving equipment, or that lifesaving equipment or its performance contributed in any way to this casualty. The conditions of the lifeboats recovered indicates that the boats were torn away from their chocks, grips and falls. The condition of the life rafts recovered indicates that they were released from their float-free racks and inflated as they were designed to. One raft was damaged, partly when it floated onto the rocky shoreline and partly by a search party which punched holes in it to allow water to drain out during the recovery operation.

Testimony of witnesses indicates that a successful launching of a lifeboat would have been extremely difficult in the weather and sea conditions which prevailed at the time *Fitzgerald* was lost. This testimony also indicates that Great Lakes mariners have little confidence that lifeboats could be launched successfully in other than moderate wind and sea conditions, and given the choice, they would use the inflatable rafts as the primary means of abandoning a sinking ore carrier. Their confidence in the capability of the rafts was tempered by stated beliefs that a raft could not be boarded safely once it was launched and waterborne and that they would inflate it on deck and wait for it to float free from the sinking vessel. This illustrates that although Great Lakes mariners understand the difficulties inherent in disembarking from a stricken vessel their level of understanding of the use and capability of inflatable life rafts is inadequate. In the opinion of the Marine Board, the appraisal by crewmen that they have small chance of survival on abandoning a stricken vessel in a rough seaway could influence them to stay with the stricken vessel rather than attempt abandonment.

The present requirement for posting a placard containing life raft launching instructions is not considered sufficient to train crew members in the proper use of this primary lifesaving equipment. The placard is, however, considered a valuable aid in assisting and reinforcing other crew training. Lifeboat drills were held on *Fitzgerald* during the 1975 season, but were not held on a weekly basis as required by regulations. The level of training of the crew in the use of lifeboats and life rafts is indeterminate.

There is no evidence to indicate that any of the crew members of *Fitzgerald* escaped from the vessel at the time of its loss. However, if they had, their chances of survival would have been significantly enhanced if they had been provided with equipment to protect them against the elements.

9. The 29 crewmen on board *Fitzgerald* are missing and presumed dead.

10. It was fortunate that the Steamer *Arthur M. Anderson* was in the area of and in radiotelephone communication with *Fitzgerald* on the afternoon and evening of 10 November. Without the presence of this vessel, the loss of

Fitzgerald would not have been known for a considerable period of time, possibly not until the following day and, at the latest, when the vessel failed to arrive at the unloading dock.

11. The testimony of witnesses indicates a conflict as to the time that the Coast Guard was first notified of the problems with *Fitzgerald*. The Marine Board concludes that the first notification that the Coast Guard received of the problem with *Fitzgerald* was at approximately 2025 (8:25 p.m.) Eastern Standard Time on 10 November in a radiotelephone call from Captain Cooper, Master of *Anderson*. At the time of his call, the actual loss of *Fitzgerald* was neither comprehended by Captain Cooper nor conveyed to the Coast Guard. The Coast Guard radio watchstander who received the call attempted to communicate with *Fitzgerald*, without success, and advised the Rescue Coordination Center. The second call from Captain Cooper to the Coast Guard, at approximately 2100 (9 p.m.), 10 November, did express a grave concern that *Fitzgerald* was lost, and rescue efforts were initiated. It is concluded that the time period which elapsed in evaluating and reporting the loss of *Fitzgerald* did not contribute to the casualty or high loss of life, because *Fitzgerald* sank suddenly, with all hands trapped on board.

12. In the opinion of the Marine Board, in a tragedy of this magnitude, occurring, as this one did, in extreme weather conditions, vessels in the area and SAR aircraft must be relied upon as the first source of assistance.

The response by the merchant vessels in the area to the Coast Guard's request for assistance was in keeping with the finest traditions of mariners. The response of the vessels *Arthur M. Anderson* and *William Clay Ford* is considered exemplary and worthy of special note. These vessels proceeded to the scene on the night of 10 November and searched under conditions of extreme weather and seas on 10 and 11 November. The response of the Canadian vessel *Hilda Marjanne*, which got under way, but was forced back by weather, is also worthy of note.

The response by Coast Guard SAR aircraft from Air Station Traverse City was timely. The first aircraft was not launched until 51 minutes after it was ordered because it was necessary to load flares for the night search. The launching of three aircraft within one hour and thirty-five minutes is within the response requirements called for by the Ninth Coast Guard District SAR Plan. The request for and dispatch of additional SAR aircraft from Coast Guard Air Station Elizabeth City, NC, from the U.S. Navy, from the Michigan Air National Guard, and from Canadian SAR forces was also timely.

The only Coast Guard surface unit in an SAR standby status which was close enough to respond within a reasonable time and was large enough to cope with the weather and sea conditions which prevailed at the time was the Buoy Tender *Woodrush* at its home port in Duluth, MN. *Woodrush*, on a six-hour standby status, was under way within two and one-half hours. The Marine Board concludes that the response by the *Woodrush* was timely. The wind and sea conditions precluded the use of the Harbor Tug *Naugatuck* stationed at Sault Ste. Marie, which had operating limitations imposed on its use outside harbor waters. The small craft designed for coastal operations which were available in Lake Superior were unsuitable for search 15 miles off shore in the high sea state then existing. It is concluded that there is a need for additional surface forces with SAR capability to improve the overall search and rescue posture in Lake Superior.

13. Because *Anderson* was following *Fitzgerald*, providing navigational assistance and observing *Fitzgerald* to be on a trackline heading for the entrance to Whitefish Bay and because the wreckage was found on a trackline headed for the entrance to Whitefish Bay, it is concluded that the outages of Whitefish Point light and radio beacon did not contribute to the casualty.

14. The progress of the severe storm which crossed Lake Superior on 9 and 10 November was adequately tracked by the National Weather Service and the weather reports and weather forecasts adequately reflected its path and severity. Weather forecasts were upgraded in a timely manner and a special warning was issued. Estimates of wind velocity by persons on vessels in the storm were higher than those forecast and also higher than those reported by shoreside stations, however, the overall severity of the storm was generally as forecast and reported. It is concluded that mariners on Lake Superior on 10 November were adequately warned of the severe weather and that the Master of *Fitzgerald* was aware of the severity and location of the storm.

15. Testimony of licensed Great Lakes mariners indicates the cargo hold of a Great Lakes ore carrier cannot be dewatered if it is loaded with a cargo of taconite pellets. The Marine Board is unable to determine the validity of this as a general proposition or whether it affected the loss of *Fitzgerald*.

16. The Loading Manual which was developed for *Fitzgerald* did not comply with the requirements of the Load Line Regulations. Since the only loading information available to the Marine Board is the total cargo carried on downbound voyages, whether *Fitzgerald* was ever subjected to unacceptable stresses cannot be determined.

17. The underwater survey of the wreckage and the detailed study of the photographs taken show no apparent relationship between the casualty and the discrepancies found and reported at the Spar Deck Inspection conducted on 31 October 1975.

18. The hydrographic survey performed by CSS *Bayfield* basically confirmed the data indicated on chart L.S. 9 and Canadian chart 2310. In addition, this survey showed that the northern end of the shoals north of Caribou Island extends approximately one mile further east than indicated on Canadian chart 2310.

19. The nature of Great Lakes shipping, with short voyages, much of the time in very protected waters, frequently with the same routine from trip to trip, leads to complacency and an overly optimistic attitude concerning the extreme weather hazards which can and do exist. The Marine Board feels that this attitude reflects itself at times in deferral of maintenance and repairs, in failure to prepare properly for heavy weather, and in the conviction that since refuges are near, safety is possible by "running for it." While it is true that

sailing conditions are good during the summer season, changes can occur abruptly, with severe storms and extreme weather and sea conditions arising rapidly. This tragic accident points out the need for all persons involved in Great Lakes shipping to foster increased awareness of the hazards which exist.

20. There is no evidence of actionable misconduct, inattention to duty, negligence, or willful violation of law or regulation on the part of licensed or certified persons, nor evidence that failure of inspected material or equipment, nor evidence that any personnel of the Coast Guard, or any other government agency or any other person contributed to the cause of this casualty.

Recommendations

It is recommended:

1.That Part 45 of Title 46 of the United States Code of Federal Regulations (Great Lakes Load Lines) be amended immediately to rescind the reduction in minimum freeboard brought about by the 1969, 1971 and 1973 changes to the Load Line Regulations.

2. That any subsequent amendments to the Great Lakes Load Line Regulations as they apply to ore carriers, such as *Fitzgerald*, reflect full consideration of the necessity for a means of detecting and removing flooding water from the cargo hold and for watertight subdivision of the cargo hold spaces. Such an appraisal should take due cognizance of:

a. The severe weather and sea conditions encountered by these vessels and the resulting high degree of deck wetness, and,

b: The inherent difficulty in meeting and maintaining a weathertight standard with the system of hatches, coamings, covers, gaskets and clamps used on *Fitzgerald* and many other Great Lakes vessels.

3. That the owners and operators of Great Lakes ore carrying vessels undertake a positive and continuous program of repair and maintenance to insure that all closures for openings above the freeboard deck are watertight, that is capable of preventing the penetration of water into the ship in any sea condition. This program should include frequent adjustment of hatch clamping devices and vent closures and prompt repair of all hatches, coamings, covers and clamping devices found damaged or deteriorated.

4. That Part 45 of Title 46 of the United States Code of Federal Regulations be amended to require closing and securing of hatches when under way in open waters and closing of vent caps when under way in a loaded condition. A visual inspection of the closure of hatch covers and vent caps should be conducted and logged by a licensed officer prior to sailing in a loaded condition.

5. That the Coast Guard undertake a program to evaluate hatch closures presently used on Great Lakes ore carriers with a view toward requiring a more effective means of closure of such deck fittings.

6. That the owners and operators of Great Lakes vessels, in cooperation with the maritime unions and training schools, undertake a program to improve the level of crew training in the use of lifesaving equipment installed on board the vessels and in other emergency procedures. This program should specifically include training in the use of inflatable life rafts and afford crews of vessels the opportunity to see a raft inflated.

7. That Part 97 of Title 46 of the United States Code of Federal Regulations be amended to require crew training in launching, inflation and operation of inflatable life rafts.

8. That the Coast Guard institute a continuing program of inspections and drills for Great Lakes vessels prior to each severe weather season. The severe weather season should correspond to the Winter Load Line season, i.e, 1 November through 31 March. Under this program, just before the severe weather season began, there would be an inspection to verify that the crew had been trained in the use of the lifesaving equipment and drills would be conducted with the crew then on board the vessel. There would be a physical inspection of the Spar Deck and all critical structural and non-structural members exposed to damage from cargo loading and off-loading equipment including, but not limited to, hatch coamings, hatch covers, vent covers, tank tops, side slopes, hatch-end girders, arches, spar deck stringers, and spar deck plating. Additionally, all emergency drills would be witnessed, and alarms, watertight closures, navigation equipment and required logs would be inspected.

9. That the Coast Guard take positive steps to insure that the Masters of Great Lakes vessels are provided with information, as is required by the regulations, concerning loading and ballasting of Great Lakes vessels, and that the information provided include not only normal loaded and ballasted conditions, but also details on the sequences of loading, unloading, ballasting and deballasting and the intermediate stages thereof, as well as information on the effect upon the vessel of accidental flooding from damage or other sources.

10. That the Coast Guard complete, as soon as possible, the studies, currently underway, which concern primary lifesaving equipment, its launching, and disembarkation from stricken vessels. And, that measures be implemented promptly to improve the entire abandon ship system, including equipping and training personnel, automatic launching of equipment and alerting rescue forces.

11. That the Coast Guard schedule maintenance status for buoy tenders and icebreakers located in the Great Lakes so as to maximize surface search and rescue capability during the severe weather season, consistent with their primary missions.

12. That Subpart 94.60 of Title 46 of the United States Code of Federal Regulations, which requires emergency position indicating radio beacons (EPIRB), be amended to include requirements for such beacons on vessels operating on the Great Lakes during the severe weather season.

13. That the Coast Guard promulgate regulations which require vessels operating on the Great Lakes during the severe weather season to have, for

each person on board, a suit designed to protect the wearer from exposure and hypothermia.

14. That navigation charts showing the area immediately north of Caribou Island be modified to show the extent of the shoals north of the island and that this modification be given the widest possible dissemination, including Notices to Mariners.

15. That the Coast Guard foster and support programs dedicated to increasing awareness, on the part of all concerned with vessel operations, inspection and maintenance, of the hazards faced by vessels in Great Lakes service, particularly during the severe weather season. The programs should make maximum use of company safety programs, safety bulletins, publications and trade journals.

16. That no further action be taken and that this case be closed.

Minimum Required Freeboard*

Date	Midsummer	Summer	Intermediate	Winter
Original	11'10³/₄"	12'6³/₄"	13'6³/₄"	14'9¹/₄"

(The above load lines were assigned when vessel was built. Authorized changes in load lines are noted below.)

3 Jul. '69	11'4¹/₂"	12'0¹/₂"	13'0³/₄"	14'3¹/₂"
17 Sep. '71	11'4¹/₂"	12'0¹/₂"	13'0³/₄"	13'2"
13 Sep. '73	10'5¹/₂"	11'2"	11'2"	11'6"

*Freeboard is the distance from the main deck to the waterline

Appendix B

Captain Cooper's Words

A decade after the sinking of the Edmund Fitzgerald, *Captain Jesse B. Cooper of the SS* Arthur M. Anderson, *the last ship to see the* Fitzgerald, *presented this document in handwritten form to James R. Marshall. It relates his experiences on the fateful night of November 10, 1975. A slightly edited version of this document was published in Mr. Marshall's* Shipwrecks of Lake Superior, *published by Lake Superior Port Cities Inc.*

We (the *Arthur M. Anderson)* departed Two Harbors, Minnesota, on the afternoon of November 9, 1975, one of the special days on Lake Superior – just ripples on the water, sunny and warm for November.

As we departed we could see the *Edmund Fitzgerald* about 10 miles astern. Shortly after we left, the weather people put up small craft warnings. By the 6 p.m. weather report, they hoisted northeast gale warnings.

As was our policy, when the meteorologists become nervous we then start our own weather plots. It did show a low pressure to the south – really didn't look as if it would become very drastic. Normal November low pressure.

As we continued east, on our run to the Soo, both the *Fitz* and *Anderson* held to the north a few miles off Isle Royale.

At this time we were having a fringe gale – 30 to 35 knots, taking spray and no green water on deck. The *Fitz,* being a faster ship, overtook us off Isle Royale.

Our midnight weather plot gave us the low's direction of movement. It should pass over the Marquette area. Still no sign of deepening. We were still having the northeast winds, being on the front side of the low pressure. It now appeared to us that we would be on the back side (of the low) for the last part of our run to (Whitefish) Bay – (with winds) over the stern.

As we approached Michipicoten Island, we had a noon plot, couldn't believe it! The low had reached Lake Superior and was intensifying dramatically. The (weather) plot told us to expect 80-knot winds on the back side. Still, the wind and sea would be astern. (We) should still make out okay.

Shortly after noon (on the 10th), we were in the eye of the storm. The sun was out – light winds, no sea.

our run to the Bay – over the stern.

As we approached Mich. Isl. we had a
noon plot, couldn't believe it! The low had
reached LK.Sup. and was intensifying dramatically.
The plot told us to expect 80 knot winds on
the back side. Still ---- the wind and sea
would be astern - should still make out O.K.
Shortly after noon – we were in the eye

The Arthur M. Anderson's Captain Jesse Cooper's handwritten manuscript described his experiences on the night of November 10, 1975.

The *Fitz* at this time was north and east of the *Anderson*. She stayed on the northeasterly course while we in effect cut a corner. We hauled for a position two miles off Michipicoten's west end. As we approached Michipicoten, the wind shifted to the west-northwest. Meanwhile the *Fitz* had passed the west end lighthouse. We started to roll. There was a dead swell from the southwest. We hauled a bit to counter the roll for a few miles, then hauled back for a position of six miles off the northeast tip of Caribou Island, a course of 120 degrees true.

As an afterthought - the *Fitzgerald* being to the east of us – the questions are: What was her course, 150 degrees? Possibly to take her in closer to Caribou Island to get what benefit she could of the lee?

As we intersected that 141-degree course for the Bay, we noted (by the heading flasher on the radar) that the *Fitz* was to the west of our course line. Maybe too close to Caribou Island.

Prior to this the last time we saw the *Fitz* was off the Michipicoten west end as it had started to snow. From this point on all the fixes (and sightings) were by radar.

(The time was) 1520 – 3:20 p.m. The *Fitzgerald* called with the info that she had a fence rail down, two vents damaged plus a starboard list. He (Captain Ernest M. McSorley) also had his pumps going, so that means that the *Fitz* had to have water in one or two of her side tanks. Possibly a stress fracture of the hull.

At this time the *Fitz* was mortally wounded. How bad we wouldn't know until later. My own opinion is that she bottomed out on a shoal. This area had not been surveyed since the 1915 era.

The wind and sea were increasing rapidly, seas running 10 to 16 feet, wind west-northwest to northwest, 40 to 45 knots. We were taking green water on deck.

The *Fitz* again called – radars out. Asked us to plot her position. We were running plots every half hour and marked her position and ours on the chart. This is a simple problem. Take a bearing on our radar of a known object or point of land. Run the oscar out (mileage gauge), bring the bearing back to true – lay it out on the chart. We then have a fix. We used our fix and projected the *Fitz* bearings the same way to give her a position.

We cleared the south end of Caribou (Island). Seas were very large, 25 to 35 feet. We were now taking a lot of water on deck, as much as 12 feet. Sometime before 7 p.m. we took two of the largest seas of the trip. The first one flooded our boat deck. It had enough force to come down on the starboard lifeboat, pushing it into the saddles with a force strong enough to damage the bottom of the lifeboat.

The first mate, Morgan Clark, on his way back to the wheelhouse, stopped in each hold to check on our watertight integrity. All was well – just a bit of condensation. The *Fitz* and the *Anderson* have identical hatch fasteners.

The second large sea put green water on our bridge deck! This is about 35 feet above the waterline!

Question: Did these two large seas reach the *Fitzgerald* at 7:10 p.m.? With a following sea, green water boarding a ship will stay on deck for a longer period of time. It would, with the increased weight of the water, increase the draft of the ship by a considerable amount. It would also pile up and stop at the forward cabins.

Morgan Clark had contact with the *Fitz* at 7:10 p.m. Still having problems, still no sign of panic or a worsening of their condition. They were holding their own.

I somehow believe this was the time of the large seas piling up forward, nosed her down, then started her plunge to the bottom. Viewing the underwater pictures, it is evident (to me) she hit a mountain on the bottom of the lake. Pictures showed many holes in her bow. If this is true, when she hit the bottom she collapsed in the middle like an accordion. The pictures showed 200 feet to be missing. Could well have torn at the area of the previous damage.

Our radars, due to the sea return on our scope, were not able to receive a clear picture close in due to the large seas which were returning an echo from the seas. The *Fitz* was entering this phenomenon on our scope, eight to nine miles ahead and to port.

A short time later (a half hour?) the snow cleared. We could see three vessels outbound from Whitefish Bay. We tried to locate the *Fitz* by phone and ships in the vicinity.

The first mate and I were at this time working both radars, using the suppressors to try and get a target. We did think at one time that we did have a faint target. It was beginning to be a grim reality that the *Fitz* was gone.

We proceeded into Whitefish Bay and with a partial lee from Parisienne Island we turned around and headed back to the suspected area.

Strange as it may seem, we had a real gung-ho sailor aft who wanted to be in a "Real Storm." He was informed by the chief engineer that we were turning around and heading back out. He went to his room, broke out the tape recorder, gave his last will and testament, sealed it in wax and put it in a jar so the world would know what happened to the *Anderson*!

After we turned, we laid out a course from our last (known) position of the *Fitz*, west-northwest from an area clear of all the shoals in the area. When we reached this line, we headed into the wind – west-northwest – hoping to find some people.

The issue of turning was not without doubts – crew, ship. What could we do if we found some of the *Fitz* crew?

At 5:30 a.m. we encountered debris – oars, life jackets, ring buoys, gas cylinders.

A bit on my crew. They manned the search light and flood lights throughout the whole ordeal. I could not have had a better group of people if I had hand picked them myself.

A few things have changed because of the *Fitzgerald* disaster. Strobe lights are now required on life jackets and ring buoys. Also, survival suits (have been developed), plus a new type of unsinkable capsule is a possibility.

Captain Jesse B. Cooper, Retired

Appendix C

Vessel Data

Vessel Name: *Edmund Fitzgerald*
Official No.: 277437
Service: Freight
Gross Tons: 13,632
Net Tons: 8,686
Length (dp): 711 ft.
Length (oa): 729 ft.
Breadth: 75 ft.
Depth: 39 ft.
Propulsion: Steam Turbine
Horsepower: 7,500
Propeller Diameter: 19'6"
Pitch (on .7 radius): 15.86'
Cargo: Taconite Pellets,
  26,116 long tons
Home Port: Milwaukee, WI

Last Inspection for Certification:
  31 Oct 1975, Toledo, OH
Last Spar Deck Inspection:
  9 April 1975, Toledo, OH
Draft (at departure on last voyage):
  27'02" forward, 27'06" aft

Owner: Northwestern Mutual Life
  Insurance Co.
720 East Wisconsin Ave.
Milwaukee, WI 53202

Operator: Columbia Transportation
  Div., Oglebay Norton Co.,
1210 Hanna Bldg.
Cleveland, OH 44115

Master: Ernest M. McSorley, Bk
  004418, License 398 598, Master
  and First Class Pilot Steam and
  Motor Vessels and GT, Master
  Great Lakes, Connecting and
  Tributary Waters, First Class
  Pilot between Duluth, Gary,
  Buffalo, North Tonawanda and
  Ogdensburg, Issue 7, 9, 29 Oct
  1973, Toledo, OH.

The Crew of the *Edmund Fitzgerald*

Captain Ernest M. McSorley, 63,
Toledo, Ohio

First Mate John H. McCarthy, 62,
Bay Village, Ohio

Second Mate James A. Pratt, 44,
Lakewood, Ohio

Third Mate Michael E. Armagost,
37,
Iron River, Wisconsin

Deck Cadet David E. Weiss, 22,
Agoura, California

Wheelman Eugene W. O'Brien, 50,
St. Paul, Minnesota, and Toledo

Wheelman John J. Poviach, 59,
Bradenton, Florida

Wheelman John D. Simmons, 60,
Ashland, Wisconsin

Watchman Ransom E. Cundy, 53,
Superior, Wisconsin

Watchman Karl A. Peckol, 55,
Ashtabula, Ohio

Watchman William J. Spengler, 59,
Toledo, Ohio

Chief Engineer George J. Holl, 60,
Berea, Ohio

First Assistant Engineer Edward E.
Bindon, 47,
Fairport Harbor, Ohio

Second Assistant Engineer Thomas
E. Edwards, 50,
Oregon, Ohio

Second Assistant Engineer Russell G.
Haskell, 40,
Millbury, Ohio

Third Assistant Engineer Oliver J.
Champeau, 51,
Milwaukee, Wisconsin

Oiler Thomas Bentsen, 23,
St. Joseph, Michigan

Oiler Ralph G. Walton, 58,
Fremont, Ohio

Oiler Blaine H. Wilhelm, 52,
Moquah, Wisconsin

Wiper Gordon E. MacLellan, 30,
Clearwater, Florida

Steward Robert C. Rafferty, 62,
Ashtabula, Ohio

Second Cook Allen G. Kalmon, 43,
Washburn, Wisconsin

Porter Frederick J. Beetcher, 54,
Superior, Wisconsin

Porter Nolan E. Church, 55,
Silver Bay, Minnesota

AB Maintenance Man Thomas E.
Borgeson, 41,
Duluth, Minnesota

Special Maintenance Man Joseph W.
Mazes, 59,
Ashland, Wisconsin

Deckhand Bruce L. Hudson, 22,
Olmstead, Ohio

Deckhand Paul M. Riipa, 22,
Ashtabula, Ohio

Deckhand Mark A. Thomas, 21,
Richmond Heights, Ohio

The Wreck of the *Edmund Fitzgerald*
by Gordon Lightfoot

The legend lives on from the Chippewa on down
of the big lake they call Gitche Gumee.
The lake it is said never gives up her dead
when the skies of November turn gloomy.
With a load of iron ore 26,000 tons more
than the *Edmund Fitzgerald* weighed empty;
that good ship and true was a bone to be chewed
when the gales of November came early.

The ship was the pride of the American side
comin' back from some mill in Wisconsin.
As the big freighters go it was bigger than most
with a crew and good captain well-seasoned;
concluding some terms with a couple of steel firms
when they left fully loaded for Cleveland
and later that night when the ship's bell rang
could it be the north wind they'd been feelin'?

The wind in the wires made a tattletale sound
and a wave broke over the railing,
and every man knew as the captain did too
'twas the witch of November come stealin'.
The dawn came late and the breakfast had to wait
when the gales of November came slashin'.
When afternoon came it was freezin' rain
in the face of the hurricane west wind.

When suppertime came the old cook came on deck
sayin', "Fellas, it's too rough to feed ya."
At 7 p.m. a main hatchway caved in
he said, "Fellas, it's been good to know ya."

The captain wired in he had water comin' in
and the good ship and crew was in peril;
and later that night when 'is lights went out of sight
came the wreck of the *Edmund Fitzgerald*.

Does anyone know where the love of God goes
when the waves turn the minutes to hours?
The searchers all say they'd have made Whitefish Bay
if they'd put 15 more miles behind 'er.
They might have split up or they might have capsized,
they may have broke deep and took water;
and all that remains is the faces and the names
of the wives and the sons and the daughters.

Lake Huron rolls, Superior sings
in the rooms of her ice water mansion.
Old Michigan steams like a young man's dreams;
the island and bays are for sportsmen;
and farther below Lake Ontario
takes in what Lake Erie can send her,
and the iron boats go as the mariners all know
with the gales of November remembered.

In a musty old hall in Detroit they prayed
in the maritime sailors' cathedral;
the church bell chimed 'til it rang 29 times
for each man on the *Edmund Fitzgerald*.
The legend lives on from the Chippewa on down
of the big lake they called Gitche Gumee.
Superior they said never gives up her dead
when the gales of November come early.

used with permission ©1976 Moose Music Inc.

Timetable for November 8-11, 1975

November 8, 1975

Low pressure system generates "a typical November storm" over the Oklahoma Panhandle, moving at 22 mph in a northeasterly track.

November 9, 1975

0700 – Storm system reported over south-central Kansas with barometric pressure of 29.53 inches (") of mercury (Hg), predicted by the National Weather Service to track south of Lake Superior.

0830 – Loading of SS *Edmund Fitzgerald* with taconite pellets commences at Burlington Northern Railroad's Allouez Dock in Superior, Wisconsin. Approximately two hours later, the SS *Wilfred Sykes* commenced loading taconite on the opposite side of the dock from the *Fitzgerald*.

1300 – Storm registers 29.40" Hg over northeast Kansas, with tracking projection amended to pass over Lake Superior.

1415 – Loading and fueling of *Fitzgerald* completed and the ship departs the dock and harbor through Superior Entry.

1630 – SS *Arthur M. Anderson* is loaded and departs Two Harbors, Minnesota, approximately 10 miles ahead of *Fitzgerald* on the normal northeastward downbound shipping lane. About this same time, the *Wilfred Sykes* departs Superior, but staying within about five miles of the Minnesota north shore.

1900 – Weather Service reports barometric pressure of 29.33" Hg as storm passes over east central Iowa, upgrading report to a gale warning, with east to northeast winds of 25-37 knots during night and north to northwest winds of 30-40 knots by afternoon on Nov. 10.

November 10, 1975

0100 – *Fitzgerald* is about 20 miles south of Isle Royale and made its routine weather report, noting winds from 030° (north-northeast) at 52 knots, 10 foot waves, visibility 2-5 miles in heavy rain. The *Anderson's* weather report substantially the same.

0200 – Weather Service revises earlier gale warning to storm warning, predicting northeast winds at 35-50 knots, becoming northwesterly at 28-38 knots later in the morning. Barometric pressure at 0100 in central Wisconsin was reported as 29.24" Hg. With this information, the masters of the *Fitzgerald* and the *Anderson* talked by radiotelephone and agreed to alter their routes to a more northerly heading to seek lee from Ontario's north shore. *Sykes* approaches channel between Isle Royale and Minnesota's north shore.

0300 – *Fitzgerald* overtakes and passes the *Anderson*, which maintains a relative position by "cutting corners."

0700 – *Fitzgerald* and *Anderson* make routine weather reports from approximately 35-45 miles north of Copper Harbor, Michigan, reporting winds of 35 knots from northeast (050º), 2-5 miles visibility, waves 10 feet. Weather Service reports storm center over Marquette, Michigan, with barometric pressure of 29.0" Hg. This is the last official weather report made by the *Fitzgerald*.

0830 – *Sykes* anchors in the lee of the Sleeping Giant inside Thunder Bay (the body of water).

0900-1000 – *Fitzgerald* and *Anderson* change course to due east, adjusting their course to track Ontario's irregular north shore.

1100-1200 – *Fitzgerald* and *Anderson* change course to track southward toward Whitefish Bay, Michigan.

1230 – The *Sykes* weighs anchor and steams for Passage Island.

1300 – Storm center over White River, Ontario, reported by Weather Service to have earlier passed west of Caribou Island. Barometric pressure is 28.95" Hg, winds shifting and gusting to 35 to 50 knots from the northwest after storm center passes. At this time, *Anderson* reports winds at 20 knots from northwest (150º) from its position 20 miles northwest of Michipicoten Island near

the storm center. The *Fitzgerald* is estimated to be about 9-10 miles ahead of the *Anderson*, but that distance opens up to 16-17 miles after the *Anderson* changes to a westerly course to "shape up" it's route through the seas north of Caribou Island where Six-Fathom Shoal is located. Heavy snows obscure an visual contact with the *Fitzgerald*.

1530 – When northeast of Caribou Island just past Six-Fathom Shoal, *Fitzgerald* master tells the master of the *Anderson* that he has a "fence rail down, vents lost or damaged and a list." The *Fitzgerald* also said he would slow or checkdown his speed and that he had "both" pumps working.

1610-1615 – *Fitzgerald* informs *Anderson* his radars aren't working, requesting that the *Anderson* keep track of them and provide navigational assistance, which was agreed to.

1700 – *Fitzgerald* requests a navigational "fix" and the mate on watch on *Anderson* relayed that information, noting the heading had the *Fitzgerald* 35 miles from Whitefish Point and 2-2¹/₂ miles to the east of that point.

1800 – Master of the *Anderson* estimates 25 foot seas 15 miles southeast and just out of the lee of Caribou Island.

1820 – *Anderson* mate calls *Fitzgerald* to request its heading, since he observes that the ship seems to be working to the left of the *Anderson's* heading. *Fitzgerald* reports steering 141 degrees True (east-southeast).

1900 – *Anderson* mate informs *Fitzgerald* its position is 1¹/₂-2 miles to the left of *Anderson* heading, 10 miles ahead, which puts the *Fitzgerald* about 15 miles from Crisp Point.

1910 – *Anderson* mate alerts *Fitzgerald* that a ship is crossing its heading nine miles ahead. *Fitzgerald* asks if it will clear the other ship and *Anderson* affirmed that it would. As the mate signs off, he asks

Fitzgerald how he is making out with its problem and the *Fitzgerald* states, "We are holding our own." A few minutes later, the snow stops and the mate is surprised not to see the *Fitzgerald* ahead of them. Three targets show on the radar, but cannot be the *Fitzgerald*. Attempts to reach the *Fitz* by VHF-FM radio fail. After several attempts, the *Anderson* calls for a radio check and is told by the responding ship that his signal is good.

2010-2235 – *Anderson* calls Coast Guard at Sault Ste. Marie, Michigan, and notifies the watchman of his concern for the *Fitzgerald*. After trying to reach the *Fitzgerald* by radio, the Coast Guardsman informed the Cleveland, Ohio-based Rescue Coordination Center (RCC) of the situation.

2103 – Clearing Whitefish Point at 2059 and still not seeing the *Fitzgerald*, *Anderson* master informs Coast Guard Sault Station that the freighter is missing. This is relayed to RCC at 2110 and CG Air Station Traverse City, Michigan, is ordered to dispatch an aircraft at 2110. By 2116, the Canadian Rescue Center at Trenton, Ontario, is notified and at 2125 the Coast Guard "cutter" *Naugatuck* (WYTM 92) is ordered to get under way from Sault Ste. Marie, Michigan, but not to proceed beyond the entrance to Whitefish Bay until the seas died down. By 2130, the cutter *Woodrush* in Duluth, Minnesota, is also ordered to get under way.

2206 – First aircraft, a fixed wing HU-16 takes off from Traverse City, after hurriedly loading flares. It arrives on the scene at 2253.

2223 – An HH-52 helicopter is launched from Traverse City, equipped with a "Night Gun," a 3.8 million candlepower, externally mounted xenon arc searchlight. It arrives on scene at 0100, November 11.

2230 (approximate) – Coast Guard requests any vessel in area of Whitefish Bay to get under way to search area.

Answering this call were the *William Clay Ford* and *Hilda Marjanne*, but the latter ship was forced back by seas. The *Sykes* and *Roger Blough*, which were downbound west of the search area adjusted their speed to join the search effort after their estimated 0300 arrival there. A bit later, the *Armco*, *Reserve*, *William R. Roesch*, *Frontenac*, *Joan O. McKellar* and *James D.* also responded.

November 11, 1975

0200 – *Anderson* arrives at search scene, having turned around after entering Whitefish Bay at approximately 2100 and being requested by the Coast Guard to return to the site.

Daybreak – An all-out search as the wind abated involves the aforementioned vessels, C-130 aircraft from the Michigan Air National Guard, Coast Guard and a Canadian rescue agency, a Coast Guard HU-16 fixed wing and two HH-52 helicopters. Shortly after daybreak, debris identified as belonging to the *Edmund Fitzgerald* was being picked up, confirming the loss of the ship, although search efforts by aircraft would continue through the 11th, 12th and 13th of November, with the search officially ended at 2213 on the 13th.

November 14, 1975

A U.S. Navy aircraft used special magnetic equipment and identified a large magnetic target on the sea bottom at almost precisely the position identified as the crash site, which later proved to be the sunken ore boat.

Glossary

AB
Able Seaman, qualified for duty as wheelman and watchman.

A.B.S.
American Bureau of Shipping, an agency that inspects and certifies ships as seaworthy and also involved in authorizing changes in load line limits for ships.

Ballast
Any weight carried aboard a ship to give it stability, but, on commercial freighters, normally understood to mean water taken into tanks in the bottom of the ship on the port and starboard sides.

Ballast tanks
Watertight compartments to the outside and below the cargo hold at the bottom of a ship into which water is pumped to add weight and give stability to a ship that is not carrying cargo. Tanks are divided at the center or keel line and designated as port or starboard. They are also divided into several tanks per side that are numbered beginning at the bow. Thus, Port No. 1 would be the tank on the left side nearest the bow.

The *Fitzgerald* had eight tanks on each side.

Beam Sea
Wind-driven seas meeting a vessel at or near 90 degrees to its keel centerline.

Boatswain (bosun)
A petty officer in charge of a ship's deck crew, rigging, anchors, cables and general maintenance other than propulsion machinery.

Bow
The forward end of a ship.

Coamings
The raised rim around a hatch opening on which hatch covers are placed, or a raised rim at the edge of a deck.

Decks
Boat: the deck at the stern of a ship holding lifeboats. Usually the highest deck at the stern and may be referred to as the poop deck.

Spar: the deck where hatches are located. Also called the weather deck.

Texas: located below the bridge or pilothouse and housing the captain's office and quarters.

Draft
Depth of a vessel's keel below the waterline.

Fathom
A unit of measurement equal to six feet. The term is most commonly used to denote the depth of water.

Flotsam
Floating debris from a shipwreck.

Following Sea
Waves driven by winds astern.

Freeboard
On ore freighters, distance from the normal waterline to the spar or weather deck.

Gagger
Great Lakes sailing jargon for extremely heavy weather.

Galley
A ship's kitchen, but often referring to eating areas as well.

Green Water
"Solid" water, as opposed to spray.

Grounding
To run aground, strike or rub bottom.

Gyrocompass
An instrument that is unaffected by magnetism and shows direction more reliably than magnetic compasses.

Hatches
The openings through which cargo is taken into the hold of a ship.

Hatch Covers
On modern ore carriers, a single large, shaped steel plate that attaches to and completely covers hatch coamings.

Heave-to
To hold a vessel so it heads toward the wind and waves, with power or sails adjusted so it maintains its approximate position; sometimes aided by a parachute like sea anchor streamed forward.

Hull
The main structure or body of a ship.

Hull Plating
The outer "skin" of a vessel, the watertight external shell. May also be called shell plating.

Keel
The principal structural member running the entire length of a ship's bottom that supports the framework and structure of the ship.

Keelson
Longitudinal interior structural beams or plates fastened over and along the keel to add strength to the hull.

Knot
A speed measurement, nautical miles per hour. A nautical mile is 1.15 statute miles. On the Great Lakes, the term "knot" is primarily used to designate wind velocity, since distance and speed are logged in statute miles.

Lay-up
Generally refers to the end of the season when ships are idled until ice goes out in the spring.

Lee
An area sheltered from the wind or waves, usually by a land mass or breakwater, but a large vessel may offer lee to another craft by positioning itself between the wind/seas and the craft being aided.

List
Usually an undesirable situation in which the ship leans to one side or the other.

Master
The chief officer of a ship, captain.

Pilothouse
The uppermost enclosed deck of a ship where the helm is located. Previously, the pilothouse was almost always at the bow, but newer boats nearly always have it at the stern.

Poop Deck
The raised deck at the stern of a ship.

Port
The left side of a ship when facing the bow.

Quartering Sea
Waves coming from an angle between amidships and dead astern, either from port or starboard.

Quarters
The room assigned for a sailor to stow his or her personal gear and sleep.

RPMs
The number of revolutions the propeller spins each minute.

Self-Unloader
A bulk cargo vessel equipped with a conveyor belt running along the bottom of the cargo hold, carrying material (ore, coal, limestone, etc.) to an elevating conveyor, which deposits it on a belt that carries it ashore on a boom reaching to the wharf.

Ship Watcher
A person hired to tend a ship during periods when it is idle (usually winter). Generally required for insurance purposes.

Shoal
An area of shallow water, a reef, sand bar or other bottom structure rising near the surface.

Shoaling
To strike or pass so closely over a shoal that damage occurs to the hull of a ship.

Six-Fathom Shoal
An area extending north from Caribou Island in eastern Lake Superior with water as shallow as 24 feet.

Starboard
The right side of a ship when facing the bow.

Steering Pole
The spar at the bow pointing directly forward and visible as a point of reference to mates and wheelmen in the pilothouse.

Steward
A cook aboard a Great Lakes ship.

Stern
The rear of a ship, sometimes referred to as "aft."

Taconite Pellets
A form of unsmeltered iron that is concentrated from lower grade ore to increase iron content to about 65 percent. This powdery ore is then formed into half-inch pellets for shipment.

Weather deck
The principal deck that contains hatch openings, also called the spar deck.

Wheel
In Great Lakes vernacular, this term has several possible meanings. "To wheel" is to steer the ship and "wheel" may refer to either the helm or, less commonly, a propeller.

Endnotes

CHAPTER 1

[1] James R. Marshall, *Shipwrecks of Lake Superior*, 1987, Lake Superior Port Cities Inc., Duluth, Minnesota, pp. 49-59

[2] *LCA Bulletin*, September, October, November, 1977, Lake Carriers' Association, Cleveland, Ohio

[3] Marshall, *Shipwrecks of Lake Superior*, pp. 60-61

CHAPTER 5

[4] Dr. Julius Wolff, *Lake Superior Shipwrecks*, 1990, Lake Superior Port Cities Inc., pp. 217-229

[5] Larry Oakes, *Star-Tribune*, November 10, 1997, Minneapolis, Minnesota, p. A1

[6] Discovery Deposition of George H. Burgner, taken Dec. 13, 1977, in Minneapolis, Minnesota, U.S. District Court for Northern Division of Ohio, Eastern District, unnumbered

[7] Burgner deposition.

CHAPTER 6

[8] Frederick J. Shannon, "Does Expedition '94 to the *Edmund Fitzgerald* Solve the Mystery of the Greatest Inland Wreck in the World?" *Michigan Natural Resources Magazine*, Dec. 1995, pp. 22-27

[9] Frederick Stonehouse, *The Wreck of the* Edmund Fitzgerald, 1996, Avery Color Studios, Marquette, Michigan, pp. 211-218

[10] Dr. Julius F. Wolff Jr., *Lake Superior Shipwrecks*, 1990, Lake Superior Port Cities Inc., Duluth, Minnesota, pp. 217-227

[11] Discovery Deposition of George H. Burgner, taken Dec. 13, 1977, in Minneapolis, Minnesota, U.S. District Court for Northern Division of Ohio, Eastern District

[12] Burgner deposition.

[13] Burgner deposition.

[14] Wolff, *Lake Superior Shipwrecks*, pp. 217-227

[15] Larry Oakes, *Star-Tribune*, November 10, 1997, Minneapolis, Minnesota, p. A1,

[16] John W. Peck, *Anchor News*, July-September 1995, Wisconsin Maritime Museum, Manitowoc, p. 45

CHAPTER 8

[17] Marshall, *Shipwrecks of Lake Superior*, p. 60

Bibliography

BOOKS

Marshall, James R., *Shipwrecks of Lake Superior*, 1987, Lake Superior Port Cities Inc., Duluth, Minnesota, pp. 49-61.

Stonehouse, Frederick, *The Wreck of the* Edmund Fitzgerald, 1996, Avery Color Studios, Marquette, Michigan.

Wolff, Dr. Julius F. Jr., *Lake Superior Shipwrecks*, 1990, Lake Superior Port Cities Inc., Duluth, Minnesota, pp. 217-229.

PERIODICALS

Oakes, Larry, "The Mystery of the *Fitzgerald,*" *Star-Tribune*, Minneapolis, Minnesota, November 10, 1997, Page A1,

Shannon, Frederick J., "Does Expedition '94 to the *Edmund Fitzgerald* Solve the Mystery of the Greatest Inland Wreck in the World?" *Michigan Natural Resources Magazine*, Bingham Hills, Michigan, November/December 1995, pp. 25-27.

Stonehouse, Frederick, "The Legend Lives On, *Edmund Fitzgerald* 20 Years Later," *Lake Superior Magazine*, Duluth, Minnesota, October-November 1995, pp. 19-27.

Trimble, Paul, U.S.C.G. Vice Admiral (Ret.) and President, Lake Carriers' Association, Letter (Sept. 16, 1977) to National Transportation Safety Board, published in the October-December 1977 Lake Carriers' Assn. *Bulletin*, Cleveland, Ohio.

PUBLIC DOCUMENTS AND COLLECTIONS

Burgner, George H., Discovery Deposition taken Dec. 13, 1977, in Minneapolis, Minnesota, under rules of civil procedure of the United States District Courts for the Northern District of Ohio, Eastern Division.

Marine Board Casualty Report: SS *Edmund Fitzgerald* Sinking in Lake Superior on 10 November 1975 with loss of life, issued July 26, 1977.

Index

About the Author

Making his home in Two Harbors, Minnesota, and maintaining an interest in almost everything having to do with the North American mid-continent, Hugh Bishop first encountered Captain Dudley Paquette in 1995 on the 20th anniversary of the wreck of the *Edmund Fitzgerald.* Growing slowly at first, the resulting collaboration was first considered to be grist for a feature story in *Lake Superior Magazine,* but got out of hand and produced a book-length manuscript.

Hugh E. Bishop

Weaving Captain Paquette's personal observations of the November 9-10, 1975, storm that sank the *Fitzgerald* with information from a variety of other sources, Bishop presents a graphic shipboard picture of a monumental Lake Superior storm, as well as the background, experience and innermost thoughts of a man who rose to the highest pinnacle of his profession and made the choice to sail in that storm.

Bishop is senior writer at Lake Superior Port Cities Inc., regularly writes for *Lake Superior Magazine* and takes a good deal of pride in having been able to continue writing for a living for nearly 35 years in northern Minnesota. He and wife, Liz, have three children.

Also from Lake Superior Port Cities Inc.

Julius F. Wolff Jr.'s Lake Superior Shipwrecks
Hardcover: ISBN 0-942235-02-9
Softcover: ISBN 0-942235-01-0

Shipwrecks of Lake Superior by James R. Marshall
Softcover: ISBN 0-942235-00-2

Lake Superior Journal: Views from the Bridge by James R. Marshall
Softcover: ISBN 0-942235-40-1

Haunted Lakes by Frederick Stonehouse
Softcover: ISBN 0-942235-30-4

Haunted Lakes II by Frederick Stonehouse
Softcover: ISBN 0-942235-39-8

Shipwreck of the Mesquite by Frederick Stonehouse
Softcover: ISBN 0-942235-10-x

The Superior Way, Second Edition by Bonnie Dahl
Spiralbound: ISBN 0-942235-14-2

Michigan Gold, Mining in the Upper Peninsula by Daniel R. Fountain
Softcover: ISBN 0-942235-15-0

*Wreck Ashore, The United States Life-Saving Service
on the Great Lakes* by Frederick Stonehouse
Softcover: ISBN 0-942235-22-3

Shipwrecks of Isle Royale National Park by Daniel Lenihan
Softcover: ISBN 0-942235-18-5

The Illustrated Voyageur by Howard Sivertson
Hardcover: ISBN 0-942235-43-6

Tales of the Old North Shore by Howard Sivertson
Hardcover: ISBN 0-942235-29-0

Lake Superior Magazine (Bimonthly)

Lake Superior Travel Guide (Annual)

Lake Superior Wall Calendar (Annual)

Lake Superior Wall Map

For a catalog of the entire Lake Superior Port Cities collection of books
and merchandise, write or call:

Lake Superior Port Cities Inc.
P.O. Box 16417
Duluth, Minnesota 55816-0417
USA

218-722-5002
888-BIG LAKE (244-5253)
FAX 218-722-4096

E-mail: nightthefitz@lakesuperior.com
Website: www.lakesuperior.com